For Maija, who was brave and funny, and who taught me to love the past. Swim on home.

CONWAY
Bloomsbury Publishing Plc
50 Bedford Square,
London, WC1B 3DP, UK
29 Earlsfort Terrace,
Dublin 2, Ireland

BLOOMSBURY, CONWAY
and the Conway logo are
trademarks of Bloomsbury
Publishing Plc

First published in
Great Britain 2022

Copyright © Strawberry
Blond TV, 2022

Strawberry Blond TV
have asserted their right
under the Copyright,
Designs and Patents Act,
1988, to be identified as
Author of this work

For legal purposes
the Acknowledgements
on p. 253 constitute
an extension of this
copyright page

Bloomsbury Publishing Plc
does not have any control
over, or responsibility for,
any third-party websites
referred to or in this book.
All internet addresses given
in this book were correct at
the time of going to press.
The author and publisher
regret any inconvenience
caused if addresses have
changed or sites have ceased
to exist, but can accept no
responsibility for any
such changes

A catalogue record for
this book is available from
the British Library

Library of Congress
Cataloguing-in-Publication
data has been applied for

ISBN:
HB: 978-1-8448-6626-7;
ePub: 978-1-8448-6625-0;
ePDF: 978-1-8448-6624-3

10 9 8 7 6 5 4 3 2 1

Typeset in FreightText Pro
Designed by Austin Taylor
Printed and bound in
Great Britain by Bell & Bain

FSC
MIX
Paper from
responsible sources
www.fsc.org   FSC® C007785

To find out more about
our authors and books visit
www.bloomsbury.com and
sign up for our newsletters

The interpretations in
this book have been drawn
in part from archaeological
excavation reports that are
the property of Solstice
Heritage.

This book accompanies
the television series
The Great British Dig
first broadcast on
More4 in 2020.

Producer
Hannah Smith

Series Producers
Audrey Neil, Lucy Malins

Executive Producer
Steve Wynne

STRAWBERRY
BLOND TV

THE GREAT BRITISH
DIG

DR CHLOË DUCKWORTH

FOREWORD BY HUGH DENNIS

CONWAY

LONDON · OXFORD · NEW YORK · NEW DELHI · SYDNEY

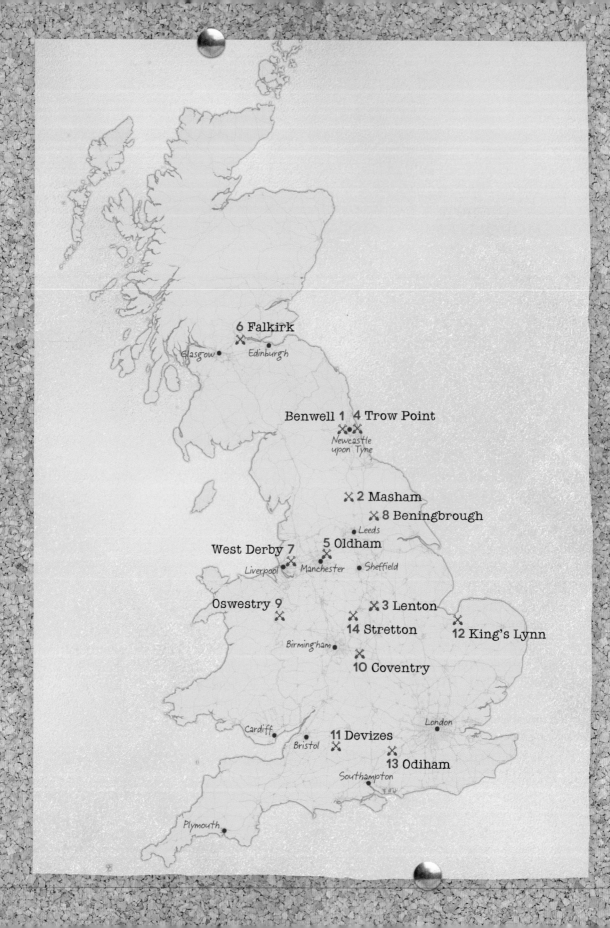

CONTENTS

Dr Chloë Duckworth
ARCHAEOLOGIST, NEWCASTLE UNIVERSITY

Natasha Billson
ARCHAEOLOGIST

Richard Taylor
ARCHAEOLOGIST

Hugh Dennis
THAT FUNNY BLOKE OFF RADIO FOUR

FOREWORD

Let's face it. This is the bit of a book that nobody ever reads,
and I have to say that in this instance I completely agree with them.

You see, as the presenter of *The Great British Dig*, a job I feel
very privileged to hold, I should be telling you about the profound
way in which archaeology allows people to connect with the
often-unexpected history of the places in which they live.

I should be regaling you with stories of the brave
homeowners who fearlessly let us on to their property to discover
the secrets underneath their lawns: of the man in Benwell, Newcastle,
who found a Roman wall under his children's trampoline; of the
headmistress in Stretton who discovered an Iron Age
roundhouse under the school playing field.

I should be praising the skill of the amazing archaeologists,
experts and historians who were able to read the clues in the
stratigraphy, brick, stone, glass, pottery, animal bone, and landscape
that enabled us to reconstruct the villas, manor houses, gardens,
and castles of the past, all now buried beneath the estates and
residential areas of modern Britain.

I should be doing all that, but honestly, that would just delay
you, and if there is one thing *The Great British Dig* has taught me
and everyone involved in it, there are far more interesting
things to be doing out in your garden!

HUGH DENNIS

INTRODUCTION

Welcome to the Great British Dig! You are about to embark upon a journey through time as we visit local communities and uncover the mysteries that lie beneath their gardens. Oh, and if you're keen to try your hand at archaeology, I can teach you how, with a step-by-step guide to excavating an archaeological trench in your own garden. Throughout the book you will also discover a series of handy identification guides to the more common archaeological finds. So buckle up, and get ready to take a grand tour through time.

THE ARCHAEOLOGY OF BRITAIN

Britain wasn't permanently occupied until about 12,000 years ago, but the discovery in 2013 of 900,000-year-old footprints in Norfolk showed that our early human ancestors quite literally dipped their toes in from time to time. In this period sea levels were much lower, and so what are now the British Isles were connected by a land bridge to continental Europe. Mobile hunter-gatherer groups intermittently occupied parts of the region during warmer periods.

Fossil evidence from around 500,000 years ago shows that our hominid ancestors hunted rhinos, elephants and hippopotamuses in southern Britain, before the advance of glaciers around 180000 BC

led to them getting cold feet, and leaving. From around 60000 BC, first Neanderthals and then modern Homo sapiens visited Britain again, developing more advanced stone tools and creating cave art at sites such as Creswell Crags on the Derbyshire-Nottinghamshire border. Mesolithic hunters knapped stone to create sharp blades and other tools, for hunting and fishing with. Farming arrived in Britain around 6,500 years ago. Early farmers constructed enormous earthworks such as henges and burial mounds, and erected standing stones at important locations, leaving a powerful imprint on the landscape that survives to this day.

From around 2200 BC, Britain's rich metal resources became important, especially Cornish tin, which was traded

Mesolithic 'microliths', small prehistoric stone tools found at Star Carr in Yorkshire

Evolution of the skull

Australopithecus
2 to 3 million years ago

Homo Erectus
750,000 years ago

Homo Sapiens Neanderthalensis
100,000 to 400,000 years ago

Homo Sapiens
40,000 years ago to the present

Inside West Kennet Long Barrow, Wiltshire

far afield to be alloyed with copper, creating bronze tools and weapons. By the time people were using iron (around 750 BC), Britain was divided into large, hierarchical groups, and particular individuals were able to amass vast amounts of wealth and power,

Iron Age fortified ruins, Broch of Gurness, Orkney

leaving behind impressive weapons and elaborate items of jewellery.

Many ordinary people lived in roundhouses and were farmers, practicing a pagan religion. The Roman conquest in AD 43 was bloody and brutal, but it was followed by a long period of peace for those parts under Roman rule. The Roman army constructed a network of roads, many of which have remained major routes to this day. Sophisticated villas and bathhouses were built, with complex heating systems (no doubt much appreciated in the harsh British winter), and the defensive forts along the frontiers became hubs of trade.

Archaeology has put to bed the old idea of the 'Dark Ages' after the Romans left Britain in AD 410. Finds such as

Roman baths at Bath, Somerset

Ruins of Lindisfarne Abbey, Northumberland

those within the magnificent 6th and 7th century burial mounds at Sutton Hoo show that people were well-connected with continental Europe, and had access to technologically sophisticated goods. Christianity had arrived at the end of the Roman period in the 4th century AD, but it wasn't until the 6th century that it really began to take hold. Then, from the late 8th century, Vikings raided much of the British coastline, famously sacking wealthy Christian monasteries such as the Holy Island of Lindisfarne. Later, however, many Vikings from Norway and Denmark chose to settle here and many took up Christianity.

After William the Conqueror invaded with a Norman army in 1066, castles were built across the land, first from timber

Burial Mound at Sutton Hoo, Suffolk

Castell Conwy (Conwy Castle), Conwy

and earthworks, and later out of stone. Churches and cathedrals were constructed as symbols of both divine and earthly power, and were often elaborately decorated, with superior masonry and stunning stained glass windows.

Bricks were costly building materials at the time, being made by hand, and surviving buildings such as the 16th-century Hampton Court Palace illustrate the beauty and complexity of early brickwork. Brick was an increasingly common building material from the 18th century, and by the mid-19th century was mass produced to support the construction of bridges and tunnels required for Britain's new railway network.

The Victorians were avid consumers, and they often discarded their waste by burying it in the garden. If you are lucky enough to have a house that dates back to the 19th century, you might find anything from medicine bottles to clay pipes to butchered animal bones in your garden! But even more recent archaeology can tell us a huge amount about the lives of people in the past, from Edwardian coins to 1940s air raid shelters. Every find, no matter how humble, ties into this big picture and links back to an individual person somewhere lost in time; a person who touched it, used it, and eventually lost it or threw it away.

Elaborate Tudor brickwork in chimneys

TIMELINE

England and Wales

100000 BC

10000 BC

PALAEOLITHIC (OLD STONE AGE)
1 million–12,000 BP*

MESOLITHIC (MIDDLE STONE AGE)
10000–4000 BC

5000 BC

NEOLITHIC (NEW STONE AGE)
4000–2400 BC

CHALCOLITHIC/BEAKER PERIOD
2400–2000 BC

2000 BC

✕ **DIG 14**
PREHISTORIC
MYSTERIES

BRONZE AGE
2000–800 BC

Scotland

0

✕ **DIG 1**
COSMOPOLITAN
ROMANS

IRON AGE
800 BC–AD 43

IRON AGE
800 BC–AD 142

ROMAN/ROMANO-BRITISH
AD 43–410

ROMAN/ROMANO-
BRITISH
AD 142–162

✕ **DIG 6**
THE FINAL
FRONTIER

✕ **DIG 2**
MEDIEVAL LIFE
AND DEATH

ANGLO-SAXON/ANGLO-
SCANDINAVIAN/EARLY MEDIEVAL
AD 410–1066

LATE IRON AGE/
EARLY MEDIEVAL
AD 162–1093

AD 1000

✕ **DIG 7**
THE
CONQUERORS'
CASTLE

✕ **DIG 3**
REBELLIOUS
MONKS

MEDIEVAL
AD 1066–1540

MEDIEVAL
AD 1093–1603

✕ **DIG 10**
OUT ON THE
GRANGE

✕ **DIG 13**
THE
SPYMASTER'S
HOUSE

POST-MEDIEVAL
AD 1540–1750

POST-MEDIEVAL
AD 1603–1750

✕ **DIG 12**
ROYALISTS AND
PARLIAMENTARIANS

TUDOR: AD 1485–1603

✕ **DIG 8**
GARDENS
OF POWER

STUART: AD 1603–1714

GEORGIAN: AD 1714–1837

✕ **DIG 9**
POVERTY AND
REDEMPTION

✕ **DIG 11**
CRIME AND
PUNISHMENT

INDUSTRIAL
AD 1750–1900

VICTORIAN
AD 1837–1901

✕ **DIG 5**
FROM MILL TO
POW CAMP

✕ **DIG 4**
WAR AND
PEACE

MODERN
AD 1900–Present

AD 2000

(*Before present)

COSMOPOLITAN ROMANS

BENWELL, NEWCASTLE UPON TYNE

One of the most incredible things about archaeology is the story that it tells of a single place over time. I really felt this when we dug in Benwell, Newcastle Upon Tyne.

We arrived at what looked on the face of it like the sort of housing estate you can find all over Britain. Well, almost. What makes the Denhill Park Estate a bit different is the enormous Roman ditch and the remains of a gateway to a Roman fort. These parts of the complex, which make up the world-famous site of Hadrian's Wall, are today sitting innocuously enough in a well-maintained, fenced-off area between the suburban houses.

Given the presence of the ditch and the gateway, you would think that we'd be uncovering evidence of soldiers living a strict military existence. But the thing that struck me most about this dig was how much of what we discovered about the people living

Tash and I practise our sales pitch: 'Hello sir, may we interest you in some free holes?'

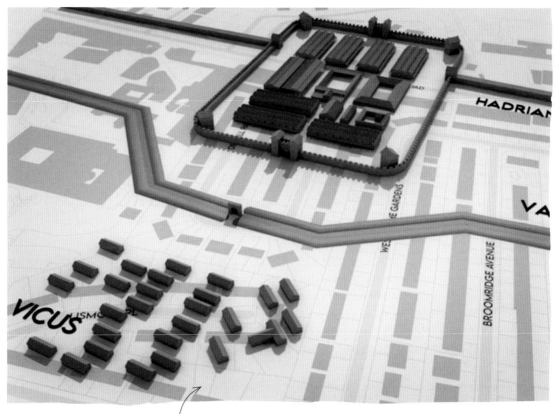

HADRIAN

VA

VICUS

WE... GARDENS

BROOMRIDGE AVENUE

Our early projection of the location of the
fort and the town, or vicus (above), based
upon the location of the ditch, or vallum, and
the entrance gate, the only parts of the fort
to survive above ground today (right)

in the area almost 2,000 years ago had in
common with today's residents.

Before the houses of Denhill Park were
built in the 1930s, archaeologists were able
to excavate a small amount of the area,
uncovering tantalising evidence for the fort
that once stood here, and throwing up some
questions we were desperate to investigate.
In particular, we wanted to know about the
relationship between the fort and the civilian
settlement that grew up around it, known
as the *vicus*.

Although it is now a quiet culdesac, the
Denhill Park Estate was once one of the 13

permanent forts that ran along the 73-mile length of Hadrian's Wall, and was one of the first forts added to the wall, between AD 122 and 126. It was built for a Roman cavalry unit of about 500 men and stayed in use until the Roman army withdrew from Britain in AD 411. That meant we were not going to find a single, Pompeii-style snapshot of life on this frontier. We were looking instead at almost 300 years of soldiers and civilians living and

For over 300 years, Benwell was one of only 13 permanent forts along the 73-mile-long stretch of Hadrian's Wall

There is something so private and personal about a back garden – digging them up appeals to my nosy side, but it's also a massive responsibility

Musing over clay pipes; the Victorian equivalent of a cigarette butt!

dying here, building and rebuilding, their changing tastes, customs and religions. To put things into perspective, that is about the same period of time that separates us today from the reign of George II, the publication of the first English Dictionary, and the so-called golden age of piracy.

There is such a sense of thrill and anticipation when you start to dig. It doesn't matter what survey work or research we have done beforehand: the only way to find out what remains is to dig it up. That also brings an element of fear, because the stakes are so high. On the first day of the dig, Tash and I knocked on the door of local resident Helen, who seemed surprisingly unconcerned about us digging up her beautiful and freshly-treated lawn. At least, until she saw us taking off the first piece of turf! I can tell you, I was desperate to find something interesting after catching a glimpse of her anxious face. In the end, though, archaeology is all about the

layers – the stratigraphy – and we were soon to discover that quite a lot has happened in this part of the world between the occupation of the fort and the 21st century.

In one garden at the end of the estate, which lies outside the wall complex, were clues to what the Victorians had been up to in these parts. Before the current houses were built in the 1930s, all of this land had belonged to one house and estate. We found 19th-century objects, including fragments of decorated clay smoking pipes. As clay pipes were relatively disposable, these are one of the most common finds of the past few centuries in archaeology. As I scraped the dirt off the surface and felt the white clay warm in my hand, it was easy to close my eyes and imagine the Victorian gentleman, surveying his estates, and flicking away his broken pipe in irritation as he pulled a fresh one from his pocket and began to pack it with tobacco.

More recent still was a rather unexpected

find made by Richard. As he started to uncover evidence for the Roman barracks, from a garden that was within the fort itself, he hit upon a second feature right alongside them: the remains of an air raid shelter from World War II. If your house was constructed during the 1930s or earlier, there is a good chance that you too have the remains of an air raid shelter somewhere in your garden, built to protect the family who lived there at the time from enemy bombers. This particular type of shelter was a mass-produced, corrugated steel version called an Anderson shelter. In the early days of the war, homeowners would have dug a large foundation trench into their garden so they could erect the steel structure, piling soil and sandbags on top to create a protected cocoon from the bombs and shrapnel. They must

Second World War air raid shelter

Wall of a Roman fort

have dug right into the Roman archaeology when they were putting it up, and I couldn't help but wonder whether they had uncovered any Roman finds and what they might have done with them.

One garden started to provide Roman finds straight away. At Tom's house, we placed our square trench within the round pit where a trampoline had been sunken into the ground in the front garden. In spite of

2,000 years of conflict: Richard found a Second World War air raid shelter jammed right up beside the wall of a Roman fort

Among the many finds from Tom's trench was a fragment of a Roman *mortarium*, with its thick body and gritty inclusions ideal for grinding and crushing food

The next time somebody complains that 'they just don't make things like they used to', show them this fragment of surprisingly modern-looking Roman glass!

looking like an alien landing pad, the lower level at which we started this trench meant that we happened upon Roman finds pretty quickly. I was especially excited as I started to wipe the soil from a fragment of colourless glass. To the untrained eye, it might look quite modern, but this was in fact really well-made Roman glass, which has survived with barely any corrosion. By comparing it with known examples elsewhere, I was able to identify it as part of a small bowl, which had been engraved with a wheel. It certainly wasn't the cheapest of items, so whoever owned it was at least comfortably well-off. More evidence for cooking and dining then popped up from Tom's trench in the form of a fragment of *mortarium*. This may sound

like an exotic and unknown item, but the clue is in the name. *Mortaria* were large, coarse bowls used for grinding in food preparation along with a heavy, handheld grinding tool: what today we would call a pestle and mortar.

Keen to find more building remains, Richard jumped in to join us in the 'trampoline trench', but he's a big bloke and frankly, he filled it, to I headed back to Helen's house! A surprise awaited me here, as we almost instantly found the trench to be rather unexpectedly wet. I was actually pretty excited about this, because it might suggest that we had hit a part of what had once been the fort's ditch. You see, when you cut a ditch into the earth, you are cutting through millennia of natural soil build-up.

ROMAN GLASS

Nothing makes you feel a connection with the past like finding some startlingly 'modern' looking artefact that dates to hundreds or even thousands of years ago. This is so often the case with Roman glass, like the fragment of a delicate little glass bowl we found under the trampoline at Tom's house.

Glass was invented over 3,500 years ago in what is now Syria, but it was the Romans who figured out how to blow it into form, and this ushered in an era of mass-produced glass for drinking, storage, lighting, and even windows; rather similar to the uses we put it to today.

Suddenly, ordinary people could afford to buy glass. This was especially exciting when it came to food and drink. That's because glass is chemically 'inert', meaning that it does not react to or absorb the contents of the vessel. Whereas metal imparts a taste to wine,

ABOVE This wall painting of a clear glass bowl filled with fruit was frozen in time by the eruption of Mt Vesuvius over Pompeii in AD 79

and even the best unglazed pottery tends to absorb the flavours of its previous contents, glass does not get in the way of flavour.

> 'You will forgive me if I say that personally I prefer glass; glass at least does not smell. If it were not so breakable I should prefer it to gold; as it is, it is so cheap.'
>
> Line spoken by the *nouveau riche* character Trimalchio, from the *Satyricon* by Petronius, late first century AD.

Roman glass windows were designed to let the light in, but not to be looked through. They were small panes of greenish or bluish glass, and were often used in Roman bathhouses, where it was important to maintain the temperature of the different 'hot' and 'cold' rooms you would pass through.

The Romans were also avid recyclers of glass. Roman literary texts speak of a 'glass peddler' who would go from door to door, collecting broken fragments of glass in exchange for sulphur. For this reason, what we find today is likely only a tiny fragment of the amount of glass in use at the time. So if you are ever lucky enough find a fragment of Roman glass, treasure that moment!

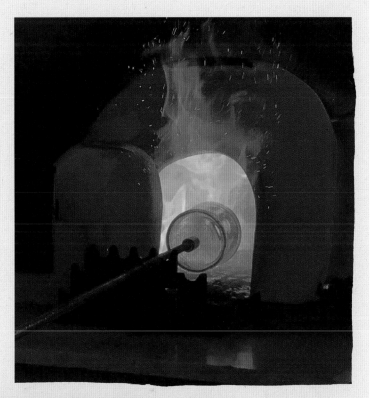

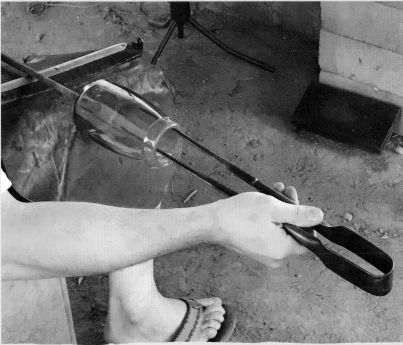

ABOVE Making and blowing glass requires specialist furnaces that consume tonnes of fuel to maintain temperatures of over 1,000°C, sometimes for days on end

LEFT Although it is rarely recognised outside of specialist circles, Roman glass was the pinnacle of the art for almost two millennia, with some designs not being successfully replicated until the 20th century

The soil you cut through will be compacted, and low in organic matter derived from dead plants and animals, which in most cases has long since rotted away. If the ditch later gets filled in, the material used to fill it will be recognisably different. This is how archaeologists can tell a ditch was once present in an area: because there will be a sharp distinction between the soil it was cut into and the soil that later filled it.

All this ditch talk may seem rather dry (if you'll forgive the pun), but ditches are actually really exciting to archaeologists. Sometimes the soil that fills what was once a ditch is completely waterlogged, meaning that it remains wet throughout the year. In such cases we have the rare chance of finding something that doesn't usually survive in the archaeological record. Items made of leather and wood, including a rare collection of Roman letters, had been preserved in waterlogged and sealed soils at the nearby fort of Vindolanda. Having promised Helen so much already, it was perhaps foolish of me to suggest she might find a Roman shoe in her garden! Now the stakes were even higher.

From then on, the Roman finds started coming thick and fast from all over the estate. Tash uncovered a fragment of fine Roman 'Samian ware' pottery imported all the way from France, and more soon followed. It seemed we were finding more and more evidence of daily life, and a fair few items that would not have come cheap! There were fragments of heavy, ceramic Roman rooftiles, a Roman coin, more pottery imported from France and from southern England, fragments of large storage vessels known as *amphorae*, and even the nail from a shoe. A particular favourite of mine – given that this fort belonged to a cavalry regiment – was a horse's tooth found within the area of the barracks blocks.

Gradually, we were starting to see a picture emerge of the fort not as some bleak, military outpost, but as a thriving community, importing fancy dining sets and glassware. I couldn't help but imagine the fort's officers and their families, using dining as a way to show off their taste in the latest fashions, and their ability to acquire exotic goods: *Come Dine with Me*, Roman-style!

We were going down deep in Helen's previously immaculate garden,

This well-paved Roman street had a sophisticated drainage system running between it and the buildings to either side

The rim of a Greyware pot. Although not as pricey as Samian ware, it had still travelled a long distance to get here, having been imported from southern England

Fancy imports like this Samian ware demonstrate that Hadrian's Wall was not a lonely, isolated frontier dotted with bleak military outposts, but a thriving band of social and commercial activity

frequently sponging out the water that filled the trench as we dug. Our efforts were rewarded when we hit upon the line of a substantial stone wall, seemingly the front of a building, and the beginning of what looked like a Roman street. We also discovered a reason for the waterlogging: there was a neat drainage channel between the street and the building front. Excited, I radioed Richard, so we could compare these findings with his two trenches.

We noted that while the remains of a barracks block he had found would have

Unfortunately, nobody had told Don never to look a gift horse in the mouth, even if you are trying to identify its tooth!

25

The community marvelled at the extent to which their gardens had changed our understanding of the fort and the vicus

been within the fort, the well-built structures found in the waterlogged trench and the 'trampoline' trench were clearly outside of it. This was no shoddy, cheaply-built affair, but a well-planned, well-constructed urban setup. What was most incredible is that we had been expecting this trench to lie in the area between the fort and the *vicus*, the civilian settlement. Instead, it turns out that the civilian settlement appears to have crept right up to the edge of the fort over time.

Remember my point about this representing about 300 years of history? We were clearly seeing some of the changes that vast time period had brought. While the fort may have started strictly as a military base, it had clearly become more of a social and economic hub over the time it was occupied. Just by opening a few small trenches in the

The current generation of archaeologists meets the next at our community event in Dig HQ

We now know that over time, the vicus crept right up to the boundaries of the fort

gardens of our obliging home-owners, we were able to redraw the map of this area.

Standing in this peaceful suburban street on a warm day, I could almost hear the sounds of the bustling Roman town, cosmopolitan as it would have been, with soldiers and other people from all corners of the Empire, including Syria, North Africa, and Rome. They ate and drank from imported table-wares, and walked along well-paved streets. Many of them would have started families with local people, and many would have chosen to stay at the end of their 25-year military service. As you will discover in Dig 6

(see page 96), a very different story awaited us when we went to Falkirk in Scotland, to investigate one of the forts on the northernmost limit of the Roman Empire: the Antonine Wall.

Local families celebrating the success of the dig, with a little nod to Roman style in their headwear!

Roman Samian Ware showing gladiators in combat

Common Prehistoric and Roman Ceramics

We can identify ceramics by examining their form (shape) and their fabric (what they are made of). Fired clays (ceramics) survive really well in the archaeological record, and because styles change over time, they can help to date the layers.

How big was the pot?

If you find a fragment from a vessel's rim, use a compass to draw a series of circles of different sizes, then lay the rim so it sits flat and figure our which circle is the best match!

Form Is it curved? How thick is it? These questions will help you to identify whether you have a fragment of a pottery vessel, tile or other object.

Ensure the rim matches completely the diameter

Wobble the rim up and down until it lies flat

Fabric After cleaning, examine the broken edge. What colour is it? Does it have inclusions or holes? Is it decorated? Has the surface been polished, painted or coated?

Inclusions like this crushed shell help to strengthen pottery and are a clue to which type you have found

Colour variation has to do with the type of clay, and how it was fired

> HOT TIP! Pottery made by hand has a slightly uneven appearance, but the potter's wheel often leaves traces in the form of regular, horizontal lines.

Neolithic Pottery

Until the Romans invaded Britain, pottery was made by coiling long rolls of clay to build the pot. A common early type found by archaeologists is Grooved Ware, dating from about 2500–2000 BC and probably first made in Orkney. Some examples have been found to have contained hallucinogenic substances.

The incisions and grooves on Grooved Ware may have imitated baskets

The colour variation in this example of Grooved Ware is evidence it was made in a bonfire, not a kiln

Bronze and Iron Age Pottery

The tools and techniques of making pottery changed little from the Neolithic to the Early Iron Age, but new forms were created.

Pottery in the Iron Age was of lower quality, and in some parts of Britain there is no evidence for pottery at all.

Beakers were associated with drinking alcohol

Roman Pottery

The Romans brought the potter's wheel, sophisticated kilns and a huge range of ceramics to Britain.

One recognisable type of Roman pottery is Samian Ware: a finely-made, bright orange import from Gaul that graced the tables of the well-to-do. You may also find Greywares, which were made in Britain.

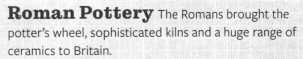

Moulded decoration on Samian ware

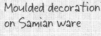

Black-burnished ware jar, 3rd century AD

GATHERING YOUR TOOLS

If you want to try your hand at a bit of back-garden archaeology, there are a few essential tools you should get a hold of, plus a whole host of non-essential but rather handy ones.

Much of what you will need can be found in your household, or bought for relatively little money. You can also raid your recycling bin, and practice some environmental sustainability at home, by reusing wooden items such as lollipop sticks and toothpicks.

Anything reasonably wide and shallow can be used as a finds tray

Your checklist

- ☐ Finds trays
- ☐ Labels
- ☐ Finds bags and permanent marker
- ☐ Washing-up bowl and toothbrushes
- ☐ Kitchen towel and cotton buds
- ☐ Wooden objects
- ☐ Spades and shovels
- ☐ Bucket
- ☐ Notebook
- ☐ String and nails
- ☐ Ground sheet / tarpaulin
- ☐ Measuring tape
- ☐ The right trowel for the job

FINDS TRAYS

You need to have somewhere to put the things you find so that they don't get lost, and you don't accidentally mix up the archaeological layers (more on this later!). I recommend having at least 4–5 finds trays. If you already own some, wide plastic seeding trays are ideal, but avoid those with compartments built into them, or those that are very shallow.

If you can, it's always better to reuse things you already have at home than to buy more plastic. Catering trays, plastic tubs that contained fruit or vegetables, or foil takeaway containers are all perfectly acceptable options. Cat litter trays are also handy, so long as you are sure to remove any existing 'artefacts' before employing them! If your trays have holes in them, be sure to have a few bags ready to house smaller or more fragmentary finds that might otherwise slip through and be lost.

It's best to label the inside and outside of the bag

LABELS

Put aside old envelopes or scrap cardboard from packaging to be reused as labels for your finds. You will need to write on these and stick them into the trays along with your finds to record which layer they belong to. While you're working, do remember to weight the labels down under a find or a stone. As any archaeologist will tell you from bitter experience, paper that isn't weighted down will almost certainly get blown away by a gust of wind at some point.

FINDS BAGS AND PERMANENT MARKER

Freezer or sandwich bags are great for storing your washed and dried finds. It's a good idea to stick your paper label in with the finds, but the outside of the bags should also be labelled with a permanent marker.

WASHING-UP BOWL AND TOOTHBRUSHES

A plastic washing-up bowl filled with lukewarm water is ideal for cleaning your finds. Old toothbrushes are brilliant for cleaning certain finds with, and this is a great way to reuse them and minimise waste.

Start saving your old toothbrushes!

A trowel: the one crucial investment

KITCHEN TOWEL AND COTTON BUDS

Paper kitchen towel is pretty handy as a surface to dry finds on, but if you prefer a more sustainable option, use some tea towels. Cotton buds are handy for cleaning any finds that are too delicate to be dunked in the water and scrubbed with a toothbrush!

WOODEN OBJECTS

A good toolkit is a balance between variety and flexibility. Lollipop sticks, wooden skewers, and cocktail sticks are all super useful for excavating small or delicate finds. Put them to one side until you have a nice little collection.

SPADES AND SHOVELS

A good spade is essential, and can be used for digging, straightening the trench sides, and – if you don't own a shovel – taking out the spoil, too. Shovels are designed to remove spoil, rather than to dig with: they are essentially giant scoops. Although many people claim to 'call a spade a spade', not everybody knows the difference between them, so if you want to avoid calling a spade a shovel, check out this 'British Gothic' photo of Tash and Richard!

Smaller hand shovels or scoops are also useful when you're working in a test pit, as manoeuvrability is limited and larger tools can get in the way.

Shovels are broader and typically more curved than spades

Spades are typically flatter and sharper than shovels

BUCKET

Buckets are not essential, but they are handy for getting rid of spoil if your spoil heap is far from the trench, and for when you reach the deeper layers.

NOTEBOOK

You will need something in which to record the different archaeological layers. Returning to the ever-present hazard of losing records to the wind, I suggest you use either a notebook, or a hole-puncher and binder to keep your notes safe.

STRING AND NAILS

These are essential for when you first lay out your trench and are also useful for recording. You'll need a minimum of four nails or pegs, and some string. The best string is very slightly stretchy, helping it to remain taut and keep the line straight.

GROUND SHEET / TARPAULIN

You will need something on which to pile your spoil until the time comes to backfill your trench. A good tarpaulin is best, as plastic sheeting has a tendency to rip.

MEASURING TAPE

You'll need at least one measuring tape for laying out and recording the trench, but it will be easier if you have two to hand.

THE RIGHT TROWEL FOR THE JOB

One essential investment is an archaeological trowel. Garden trowels are designed for digging down into soft topsoil, and are not appropriate for archaeology. A bricklayer's pointing trowel is absolutely fine, but you can also buy specialist archaeology trowels online for under £10. For its versatility, I recommend going for the 4-inch version.

You can purchase a trowel from Past Horizons, a long-lived online shop that specialises in archaeological gear: www.pasthorizonstools.com

MEDIEVAL LIFE AND DEATH

MASHAM, YORKSHIRE

'I feel quite spoiled in a way, because I know that wherever I go now, I'm not going to get this!' Richard's words at the end of our dig in Masham probably rang true for all of us. It was an incredible privilege to work here, not only because it is a warm and welcoming town in a beautiful part of Yorkshire, but because we had been tasked with finding and excavating some burials that were part of an early medieval cemetery.

Normally, of course, finding a human skeleton in your garden would be cause for phoning the police. Indeed, nobody in the UK may excavate human remains without first seeking a licence from the Ministry of Justice, and archaeologists are no exception to this rule.

The cemetery lying beneath modern day Masham dates to between the 7th and 11th centuries AD, the time period that used to be known as the 'Dark Ages' because of the

Using long, thin trenches oriented north-south, we planned to catch any signs of east-west human burial in the gardens of local residents

We all fell in love with beautiful Masham

relative lack of written history. But dark ages do not remain dark when you have archaeology on your side.

The burial site was first discovered during some plumbing works in the late 1980s. The remains of 58 individuals were excavated from the area of the works, but there was no way of knowing how far the cemetery extended. That was where we came in: by digging in the gardens of local residents, we hoped to learn more about the size of the cemetery. How many burials were still there beneath the streets of 21st-century Masham?

We were also excited at the prospect that at least some of the individuals buried here may have been Scandinavian, or had Scandinavian ancestry, following the first Viking raids in AD 793. There is a popular image of the Vikings as harrying Britain's shores and returning home with their loot, but there is another side to this story. Many of them chose to stay here, attracted by the good farmland, and some would have married locals.

As this was a Christian cemetery, we knew that the burials would be oriented east to west, so our strategy was to put long, thin trenches running north to south in the gardens of willing local residents. This way, the trench was more likely to intersect with any burials present, in which case we could open it out more to reveal the entire burial.

Initially, we didn't seem to be finding any evidence of the cemetery. My own trenches turned up a fair amount of Victorian material. This is a fairly common find in the back gardens of older houses. During the 19th century, people began to consume goods on a far greater scale than before, made possible by industrialisation and the development of factories. The world hadn't yet caught up with this explosion in material items and organised large-scale refuse collection services, so people buried their rubbish in pits in their back gardens.

Queen Victoria herself set a trend for pottery, which of course is one of the things that survives very well in the archaeological

Among the 19th and 20th century finds were a lot of butchered animal bones, bottles and jars, and a hint that somebody had lost their marbles

record, and so it is a common find in the upper layers of our trenches, along with pharmaceutical glass bottles, butchered animal bones, and various other items from the 19th and early 20th centuries. There were no human bones here, which helped us greatly with defining the limits of the cemetery.

Although she was only working across the street from me, Tash's findings were very different. She got on the radio to human bone expert Dr Lizzy Craig-Atkins, who headed down from Dig HQ. Lizzy confirmed that Tash had exposed the skull and upper arm bone of our first burial.

Excavating human remains can be an emotional experience. Nothing speaks to the beauty and fragility of life like gently uncovering the bones of a person who

died hundreds or even thousands of years ago. Personal objects hold memories for the people who own and use them, but the circumstances of your life are recorded in your very bones themselves. From childhood nutrition, to how much physical work you do, to what injuries you have suffered and various diseases that can show up in the bones, the skeleton tells a very personal story.

Through long years of experience, archaeologists specializing in human remains are also able to identify the sex and the approximate age at death just by looking at your bones and teeth. With scientific techniques such as stable isotope analysis and radiocarbon dating, we can take this yet further, working out when you died, but also where you grew up and whether

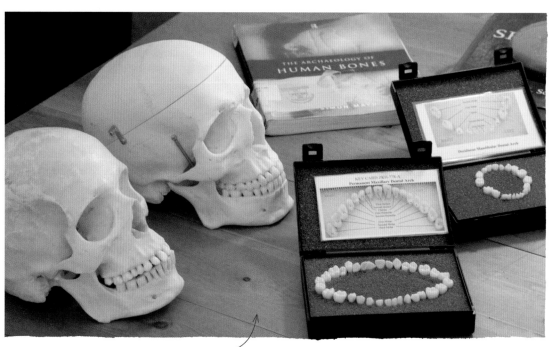

Replica skulls and teeth help human bone specialists to identify archaeological finds

you moved to a different part of the country in adulthood.

Meanwhile, Hugh went to meet facial reconstruction expert Professor Caroline Wilkinson. Caroline's work involves rebuilding the face of an individual from their skull. She starts by laying the muscle structure over the shape of the skull and follows this with the skin and facial features. Because we can determine the average age at death of an individual, it is possible to create an accurate enough reconstruction. Caroline also works frequently with the police to help identify more recent human remains. Because we can't work out skin, hair or eye colour from bones without undertaking DNA analysis, any reconstructions Caroline was to do for us this week would be in black and white.

We were soon to discover that there would be more than one contender for Caroline's reconstruction. Richard, who had been digging in the local pub's beer garden, had exposed another skeleton, in an archaeological layer just below some medieval pottery dating to the 12th century: a good sign that we had found another burial from the 7th–11th centuries. Richard was working very gently to expose the bones, while chatting to Brian, the owner of the pub.

There is an old adage in archaeology: the dead don't bury themselves. What we mean by this is that burial is really a rite of passage for the living, and that the burial of an individual tells us more about the needs of those who outlived them than it can about the wishes of that person. As Richard worked carefully to expose the entire skeleton, I couldn't help but imagine who buried this person: did they have a husband or wife, or children? What was said in farewell to them on that day?

Not to be outdone by Richard, Tash soon discovered that her trench contained

Facial reconstruction expert Professor Caroline Wilkinson tells Hugh about her fascinating work

THE WRITING'S ON THE BONES

What does your skeleton say about you?

Archaeologists who specialise in human bones are known as osteologists. We were lucky enough in Masham to have osteologist Dr Lizzy Craig-Atkins with us in Dig HQ. As she explained to Hugh, there are many ways in which osteologists are able to 'read' a skeleton. Teeth, for example, wear down at a fairly reliable rate over time, so they are an excellent indicator of the age of an individual at death. Children and young adults can also be aged based on the degree of fusion of certain bones. The pelvis is used as an indicator of biological sex because females develop wider hips during puberty, to enable childbirth.

Osteologists will clean the bones and carefully lay them out on a table. They log every bone that is present and note if any are missing (smaller bones in the feet, for example, may be moved by animals). Certain diseases show up in the bones, as can signs of traumatic injury, but most causes of death do not leave their mark on the skeleton.

What does show up really well, however, is anything long-term, particularly physical stress. Manual labour affects your bones because it requires thicker muscle attachments, so we can tell how active a person was in their life, and even understand something about the type of labour they undertook, based on which muscles were the most developed. When

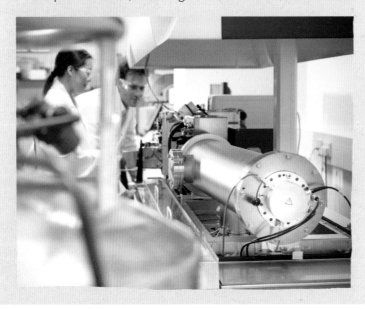

ABOVE Dr Lizzy Craig-Atkins carefully and respectfully lays out a skeleton for examination

LEFT Modern scientific techniques such as isotope analysis have revolutionised the study of human remains

osteologists examined the bones of sailors from the sunken Tudor warship, *Mary Rose*, they found that the men were relatively young, but had a lot of stress on their joints. This makes sense, because they would have spent their days heaving and hauling on ropes to operate 2-tonne cannons.

We can learn even more about a person's life by applying scientific techniques to their bones and teeth. Isotopes are atoms of an element that have an unequal number of protons and neutrons in their nucleus (core), giving them slightly different masses. Radioactive isotopes, such as ^{14}C (measured in carbon dating), are unstable due to the imbalance between protons and neutrons, and they decay over time. Stable isotopes, on the other hand, remain the same over time. Scientific techniques relying upon isotopes use a technique called 'mass spectrometry' to measure the ratio of one isotope to another in human bones and teeth, with the results reflecting where a person lived and what they ate.

For example, the ratio of ^{18}O to ^{16}O in groundwater varies across Britain and this is translated into our body when we consume the water. Different stable isotopes of carbon vary between different types of plants and between land and marine animals. By combining multiple types of isotope analysis, we can build up a picture of where an individual lived at different stages of their life, and what sort of diet they had. Archaeological scientists investigating the remains of Richard III with these techniques were able to determine that his diet became richer after he took the crown, and that the king had moved from the east to the west of the country in childhood.

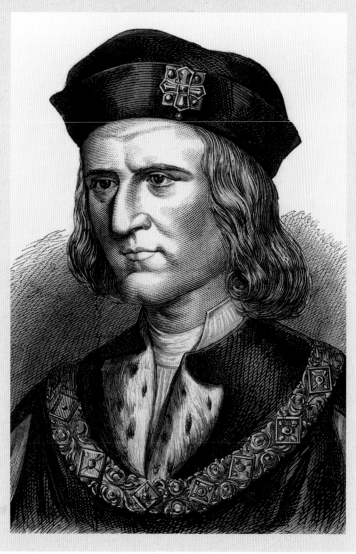

RIGHT Through osteology, DNA and isotope analysis, the skeleton of Richard III gave a wealth of information on his life and death

Richard radios Dig HQ

This well-preserved adult skeleton had lain hidden beneath the local pub garden

the burials of not one but two individuals. Through careful excavation, she was able to establish that they had not been buried together as is sometimes seen in so-called 'lovers' burials'. Rather, the person digging the later grave had cut into an earlier burial, illustrating that the cemetery must have been in use for a long time, and that – at least in places – it was quite densely packed.

Lizzy soon arrived on the scene, accompanied by local resident Roger. She was able to establish that one of the individuals was probably male, while the other was most likely a young female who died between 11 and 15 years of age. This girl was probably laid to rest within a shroud, as her fragile, gracile bones were found tightly together with her left hand over her right. It is likely that she suffered from either malnutrition or a disease earlier in her childhood, based upon horizontal lines in her teeth. These two individuals were not as well preserved as Richard's burial in the pub garden, and Tash decided to leave the smaller one in the

This slender, gracile skeleton belonged to a young female aged 11-15 years at the time she died

As Lizzy arrives, Tash extends her trench

Tash shows Lizzy her findings

Tash discusses her findings with Hugh, Richard and me

ground as removing her would have caused too much damage to the skull.

Back at Dig HQ, Lizzy was able to establish that her earlier hunch was correct and that one of Tash's individuals was male. He had a large mandible, with a strong jawline, and his teeth were very worn, suggesting that he was at least 45 years old when he died, possibly older. During this period, people ate a lot of bread and porridge, which were made from coarsely ground cereals, and it was fairly common for small stones to make their way into the mix. Such a diet wears the teeth down greatly and, coupled with a lack

Rev David Cleaves discusses re-burying excavated skeletons

of dental hygiene, meant that many people would have had tooth decay. It is likely that people had to put up with a lot of pain from their teeth. The only real solution to most problems would have been to remove the teeth, so many individuals may have ended life with rather few of them.

Richard's skeleton was the most intact, and so Caroline selected this one for her facial reconstruction work. She started by

MASHAM'S BIGGEST BIRD

One of the parts of archaeology that rarely makes it to TV is what we call 'post-ex' (short for 'post-excavation'). This is an extension of the process that takes place in our Dig HQ, in which various specialists study the materials recovered from the site, and write reports on their findings.

During her post-ex analysis of the material recovered from Masham, zooarchaeologist Dr Hannah Russ made an exciting discovery. Zooarchaeology is the study of animal bones, and Hannah's specialism is fish, on which you will learn

BELOW Finds experts carry on making discoveries long after the digging has stopped

more later. This particular discovery, however, was related to something rather different.

Hannah had her work cut out for her at Masham because we found a very large quantity of animal bones. Many of them showed signs of butchery, indicating that this was food waste. (If you find any animal bones on your dig, you can check them for signs of butchery such as sharp cut lines, chop marks or saw marks, all of which are illustrated here for comparison.) While she was cataloguing and identifying all these bones, Hannah happened upon something rather unusual in a layer of finds from the 19th century.

Her find was a partial chicken skeleton, but what made it so unusual was the size. Hannah measured the bones and compared them with several datasets on chicken bones found in archaeological contexts, as well as modern chicken bones from a range of breeds. It turns out that she had just identified the largest chicken bones *ever* to be recovered from an archaeological deposit in England!

The size of the bones were consistent with a breed of chicken known as the Brahma Chicken, extremely large birds that were imported to the UK from East Asia in the 19th century. Interestingly, the assemblage also included a second right femur (the thigh bone). This was equally large and indicated that two enormous chickens had once been buried here. None of the bones showed any signs of butchery, and the bone growth around the toes suggested that this had been a rather old bird at the time of death, which would have made it no good for eating. These facts suggest that the chickens had been kept as pets, or perhaps – given the fancy breed – for showing.

ABOVE The enormous chicken bones are consistent with a breed known as the Brahma Chicken

Lizzy shows Hugh and Brian just how much information can be gleaned from human bones, if you know what to look for

photographing the skull, while Lizzy wove together the evidence from the whole skeleton for Hugh and pub-owner Brian. As she explained, the pelvis confirmed that the individual in question was male. He also had extreme wear on his teeth, indicating either a very coarse diet or that he used his teeth as tools. Interestingly, his other bones indicated that he was younger than might be assumed based on the teeth: perhaps 30–40 years old at the time of death. As Hugh put it, we were looking at a 'youngish man with bad teeth'. This man also had fairly severe joint disease,

indicated by the lower spine, and strong muscle attachments.

Taken together, it is likely that these were the remains of a man who was engaged in heavy manual labour. Most people at this time were farmers, growing their own food, and it would have been demanding work. By the end of his life, this man suffered from joint disease and poor dental hygiene. What else he may have suffered, and what caused his death, we cannot say. But thanks to Caroline, we were able to catch a glimpse of how he would have looked.

In the moment before Caroline revealed the face of this man, who had lived a thousand years ago, you could have heard a pin drop in Dig HQ. She turned her screen, and there before us was a very handsome, surprisingly modern-looking face. Rather a

Richard's delight at seeing the face of the man whose skeleton he had so carefully excavated

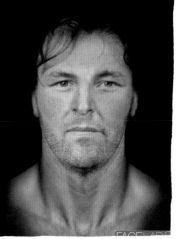

few people commented that he resembled Sean Bean, which was wonderfully appropriate given that we were in Yorkshire – a distant ancestor, perhaps? As Brian aptly put it, Caroline's reconstruction had 'put a whole new dimension on everything'. And that's what I love about archaeology: it is teamwork, a group project, and every part comes together to bring the past to life.

The bones that we removed will be reburied in Masham's cemetery, in a Christian rite to respect the wishes of the original grieving families. The young girl was gently covered over again where she had originally been laid. She was at peace.

Caroline's expert reconstruction reminded us all of how much we have in common with people of the past – after we finish studying the bones, both excavated skeletons will be returned to rest in Masham's present-day cemetery

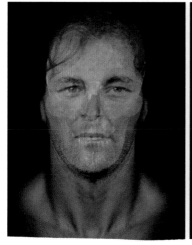

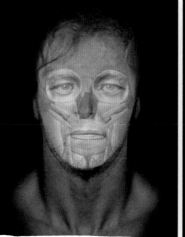

RESEARCHING YOUR LOCAL AREA

Long before any spade breaks through the turf, archaeologists spend a considerable amount of time gathering information on the site and the local area. This is vital to understanding the wider context of your archaeological discoveries, and it's also just plain sensible: putting in the background research will help enormously with interpreting what you see in the trench.

More than anything, however, documentary and archival research is great fun, and a large chunk of it can be done from the comfort of your own sofa. If you have any family members who can't or don't want to dig, but would like to be involved, this is a great role for them to take on. And you never know – they might just turn up something truly fascinating.

There is a wealth of online resources available out there if you know where to look

HISTORICAL MAPS

The best place to start any background research is with old maps of the area around your planned excavation. There is a wealth of great online resources out there, with an increasing number of local record offices and councils providing online access to their historical maps. The best place to start, however, is the huge set of maps available via the National Library of Scotland. The website provides direct access to detailed Ordnance Survey mapping for England and Wales as well as Scotland.

For most parts of the country, you should be able to get easy online access to Ordnance

New guide: Re-using our
georeferenced maps

Guide to this website

Ordnance Survey maps

Maps of Scotland

County Maps

Estate Maps

Town Plans and views

Coastal / Admiralty charts

Military maps

Series maps

Bridges / Canals / Railways

Air Photo mosaics

Bathymetrical Survey

Map Finder - with Marker Pin
Find maps using a Marker Pin

Map Finder - with Outlines
Find maps with their outlines shown

Explore Georeferenced Maps
Maps overlaid on a satellite image backdrop

Side by side viewer
Compare maps in a split-screen viewer

Browse by Mapmaker
Browse maps by names of surveyors or engravers

Roy Military Survey viewer
View Roy Map and shelfmarks for dissections

OS sheet records viewer
Find and view records for detailed OS maps (some not online)

Boundaries viewer
View boundaries for parishes, counties and unitary authorities

The National Library of Scotland provides resources that cover the whole of Britain

Maps are a useful resource

Survey maps from the mid-19th century onwards. Even without further research, this provides a fantastic insight to the development of your local area. If you're keen on a 'behind the scenes' glimpse of the wider archaeological team behind the Great British Dig, look no further than our Robin, who always arrives equipped with printouts of the relevant historical maps, to help interpret what we find. This is how we were able to link our inkwell and slate pencil with a 19th-century charity school at our dig in Falkirk (Dig 6, see page 96).

ONLINE LOCAL HISTORY

A great first port of call when looking into your local area is the Victoria County History. This is a long-running project to curate detailed historical overviews of all the counties and parishes of England. Many of the volumes are now available online and provide masses of well-researched detail for you to investigate further. Victoria County History is housed by the British History Online website, and here you can also access a vast quantity of collated historical research on Scotland, Wales and Northern Ireland.

If you have ever tried to trace your family history, you will probably be familiar with various subscription-based websites which feature large databases of information such as census records, births, marriages and deaths, tithe apportionments and mapping relating

Useful Links

The National Library of Scotland:
   www.nls.uk

The British Library:
   www.bl.uk

Victoria County History:
   www.history.ac.uk/research/
   victoria-county-history

British History Online:
   www.british-history.ac.uk

British Geological Survey Map Viewer:
   www.bgs.ac.uk/map-viewers/
   geology-of-britain-viewer

to early 19th-century land ownership, records of emigration and immigration, and military service records. Such sites often provide links to more specialist databases for those wishing to delve deeper.

LOOKING AROUND

One of the best ways to understand your local area is to go out and have a walk around, keeping your eyes peeled for older-looking buildings, unusual road layouts and even modern street names. Combined with map-based research, it is possible to unpick the development of a village or town, identifying where the oldest parts of a settlement are and understanding how it has grown and changed over time. Street names and place names in particular can provide a surprising amount of information about what preceded the creation of modern houses – check out the box feature What's in a Name? (page 53) for more on this point.

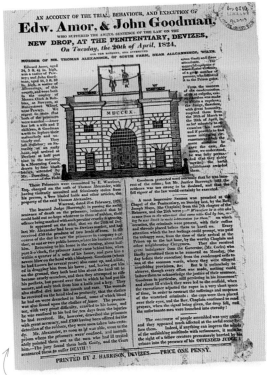

Local newspapers (such as this one from our dig in Devizes, see page 182) can provide fascinating layers of historical detail

USEFUL APPS

OS Maps The Ordnance Survey app allows you to track your location using your phone's GPS, and you can even identify and download areas of interest. Sadly, it doesn't yet include historical maps. For those, you'll need to refer to the resources mentioned above.

iGeology This app from British Geological Survey will tell you in detail what type of bedrock there is in your garden, and what lies above it (the superficial geology). Super useful if you're trying to work out whether you are in a natural layer or not, or whether you are seeing the use of imported materials.

YOUR LOCAL RECORD OFFICE

While some record offices have an online search facility, and even some online resources available, there is an absolute treasure trove of material to be investigated in hard copy within the record offices themselves. It may seem a little daunting at first if you have never stepped into an archive, but all the local record offices have experienced staff to help you with the specifics of your search and source the documentary records in which you are interested. A quick internet search should provide details of opening times and whether you need to book your attendance in advance. Manually examining archive records can certainly be a more lengthy process than online searching, but it is a real thrill to pore over the historical documents themselves and discover some brand new titbit that sheds light on your local area.

Visiting local archives can be a real thrill

3 REBELLIOUS MONKS

LENTON, NOTTINGHAM

Heading to Lenton in Nottingham felt something like going home for me, as I lived there when I first studied archaeology at the University of Nottingham. With its historic pubs, medieval street names, and secret networks of caves running under the city and castle, Nottingham is not short on archaeological potential, and the legend of Robin Hood permeates the character of the city.

Lenton was a significant place in the medieval period and was home to one of the largest and most important medieval priories in the country. Priories were monasteries, housing friars, monks or nuns who had taken religious vows. The church would have been the tallest and most impressive building of the complex, which also included dining and sleeping areas.

For more than 400 years, Lenton Priory served as the home and place of worship of Cluniac monks, until the dissolution of the monasteries by Henry VIII between 1536 and

This surviving column base gives a sense of the enormous size and grandeur of Lenton's lost priory church

Nottingham, city of caves, legends, and hidden treasures

Terri asks whether we can leave her husband Simon in the trench before we backfill

1541. The priory was originally founded in the early 12th century by one William Peverell, a favourite of William the Conqueror who had been granted extensive lands and titles by the Norman king himself. Peverell lived in Nottingham Castle, situated on an impressive sandstone promontory that afforded commanding views over the surrounding landscape. (This promontory is also riddled with a network of caves, which have been occupied throughout Nottingham's history.)

Peverell would have been able to look out and see Lenton Priory from his castle,

Community Engagement Officer Josh Pickering explains that Lenton Priory Church was visible from Nottingham Castle

and – at approximately the same size as Westminster Abbey – it must have looked stunning in its heyday. He would have built it to demonstrate his devotion to God and his King, and to make his own mark on the landscape. It certainly worked: here we were almost 900 years later, keen to discover as much as we could of this monumental undertaking.

Tash, Richard and I found Hugh sipping a pint in the local pub garden. What he

didn't know when he sat down is that he was directly above what would have been the nave of the priory church. As we left the pub and walked around the corner, we were greeted by a host of street names relating to the area's ecclesiastical history, including Old Church Street, Priory Street, and The Friary. We guided Hugh to the one surviving above-ground feature of the priory church: a broad stone column base, consistent with a truly substantial building. We were here to explore

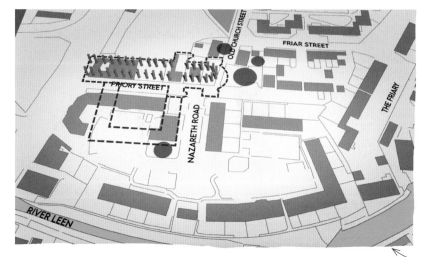

Our projection of where the priory church once stood

WHAT'S IN A NAME?

Warning: once you start to look at street names with interest, you will find it hard to stop!

Have you ever considered how the street where you live got its name? In the USA, where towns and cities were built to a grid system, many streets simply have numbers. Here in Britain, however, where space is at a premium and we tend to rebuild multiple times in the same location, the street names often reflect what was there before. This was the case in Lenton, with surrounding street names pertaining to the priory and its church, but it is also the case throughout the country. Do you know a Kiln Street, or Glasshouse Lane, reflecting the presence of now-forgotten industrial heritage?

Longer-lived street names may reflect the economic activities that took place there or, quite simply, what (or where) the street led to. They would only have become formalised with the development of ordnance survey mapping of Britain throughout the 19th century. For examples of street names reflecting economic activity, think of Market Street or Baker Street. Common street names based upon where the road leads include London Road, Mill Lane, and Station Road.

Towns and cities that have retained some of their medieval structure will often have various 'gates', stemming from a time when cities were surrounded by high defensive walls, and even smaller settlements by some less substantial form of enclosure. Often these gates were differentiated by the points of the compass so the North Gate, for example, might later become Northgate Street.

This is how place names also translated into surnames, by the way. If you were a Gareth living near the South Gate of your town, and you volunteered for work away from home, you might want to distinguish yourself from the other Gareths, and that's how you would become Gareth Southgate.

In a more extreme example of street names reflecting the economic activity that once took place there, we have the infamous Grope Lane, of which there are still examples in both Shrewsbury and Whitby. The longer version of this name is too rude for this book, and seems to have been too rude for the Victorian era too, during which such streets were almost universally renamed (for example, Magpie Lane in Oxford once had a much more colourful name, which is not too difficult to discover online). If you happen upon a Grape Lane, this is almost certainly a prurient Victorian renaming of a somewhat more infamous street!

Students George and Scott receive a lecture in archaeological finds from Anni

the east end of the church, which should have been under the garden of local residents Terri and Simon. We also wanted to learn more about the extent of the priory itself and how the landscape changed over time, especially the course of the local river, the Leen, which would have been a vital water supply for the monks, as well as an important riverine 'highway' for the transport of goods, and communication.

I have come to learn that archaeology, with its practical nature and its reliance on teamwork, can be a powerful tool for bringing communities together. This was illustrated beautifully in Lenton, where

long-term residents Terri and Simon got to know the students living in the house nearby. Because students typically take out relatively short-term rental contracts, they can often move through an area without engaging with its local community. By the end of our time in Lenton, however, Terri was promising to take them some of her delicious home cooking, and they were all arranging future meet-ups in the pub!

'Who needs lectures, anyway, when you're unearthing history?' asked student Scott, as he and housemate George worked hard to excavate a small test pit in their back garden. Thus far, they were finding a lot of material dating to the 18th and 19th centuries, including a fragment of a salt-glazed ale tankard, clay pipe stems, and oyster shells. The students seemed pretty happy with the

Chatting to the students about their 19th century assemblage of finds

idea of their predecessors smoking from their clay pipes, drinking ale from their salt-glazed tankards, and dining lavishly on oysters. But as I explained to George, oysters were not seen as a pricey foodstuff at that time and were fairly commonly eaten.

Meanwhile, Tash was directing the digger driver in an extension of the larger trench in Terri and Simon's garden. Here we were hoping to catch the east end of the priory

Examining the different layers found within the soil core

Tash supervises the digger as it extends Terri and Simon's trench

church, about which very little was known.

Richard was boring. I don't mean that rudely, of course! He was in fact using a 'borehole drill' to extract a long tube of soil from far deeper in the ground than we would be able to dig. This sort of sampling exercise is typical in archaeology when our questions extend more broadly than the confines of the trenches. In this case, we were hoping to trace the ancient course of the River Leen and hopefully identify the monks' cloisters. Borehole sampling also allows us to get a sense of the depth of the archaeological deposits: how far down would we have to dig

Buildings expert James Wright finds some worked stone in the soil core

to hit the medieval layers?

Richard shared the borehole results with medieval buildings expert and stonemason, James Wright. Archaeological finds were pulled up along with the soil in the sample, allowing him to trace the layers from modern through to post-medieval and finally the medieval period. They were also able to identify alluvium, indicating the ancient course of the river.

James noticed a piece of worked sandstone known as 'Mansfield Red' in the borehole sample. This stone was of a high quality and would have been carved elaborately and used in the finer architectural details. What we found from the borehole would be consistent with the monks' cloisters being located in this area, close to the course of the river. They would be able to make use of the water for cooking and washing, but the river would also have been used to carry away the effluent of their toilets.

I love digging medieval archaeology. The finds really speak to me, perhaps because so many of them are reminiscent of things we still make and use today. Ceramic jugs, wine glasses, keys, coins... they are at once familiar and strange. Postgraduate student Sarah was helping me out in one of our trenches when she noticed something small and green twinkling in the soil. It was a fragment of 'green-glazed ware', a typical medieval pottery type. We took it to finds specialist Anni Byard, back in Dig HQ, and she pointed out the ridges on its surface, possibly made by the potter's own fingers as it was turned on the wheel. These ridges identified it as belonging to

For medieval literature student Sarah, the green-glazed pottery was right up her street, both literally and figuratively!

Lead is a really pliable metal, making it perfect for wrapping around things and holding them in place... in this case, stained glass windows

a jug or pitcher, and that it would have dated to between about AD 1200 and 1500.

Sarah and I were delighted with our image of the monks swigging ale or mead from their attractive, glazed pitchers, but there was more to it than the personal connection. Pottery is really useful for the archaeologist because we can identify different 'fabrics' to the locations in which they were made, and different styles to the time periods during which they were in fashion. It turns out that people in the past were just as susceptible to changing trends as we are today, and just as you or I could identify a particular hairstyle or outfit to the 1980s or 1990s, the archaeological finds specialist can identify a piece of pottery to the timespan in which it was popular.

Tash had the job of explaining to Terri and Simon that she had found some disarticulated human bone in their garden. Disarticulated bones are those that are no longer together as they would have been at the time of burial, indicating that a burial was at some later point disturbed, in this case probably due to the root action of trees.

The presence of bones was not entirely unexpected, though: after all, we were excavating in the environs of a church. The eastern end of the priory church, where we were, would have been earmarked for the 'VIP' burials, as Hugh put it. These important people would have been high-ranking members of the clergy and rich benefactors who contributed to the church's coffers over time, keen to buy themselves a direct ascent to heaven. What did surprise us was the sheer number of human remains found here. It seems that the cemetery was longer-lived than had originally been assumed – yet another unexpected find from our dig in Lenton.

While we were all interested to uncover more about life at the priory while it was in use, we could not escape the dark shadow hanging over its final days. These were the times of King Henry VIII, who wished to end his first marriage to Catherine of Aragon and marry his mistress Anne Boleyn in the hope of producing a male heir to the throne. Keen to

escape the heavy digging, Hugh popped over to Nottingham's Market Square to meet with medieval historian Dr Natasha Hodgson and find out more about how Lenton Priory was entangled with these historical events.

You see, when the Catholic Church refused to grant Henry a divorce, he took advantage of the religious reform movements taking place at the time and broke from the Church. Much of the Church's wealth was bound up in religious houses such as Lenton Priory, and Henry quickly took advantage of this too, dissolving them and claiming their riches for the crown. The brave monks at Lenton Priory resisted this reform, however, and that

Tash discovered many fragments of disarticulated human bone, identified by expert Kate Smart.

King Henry VIII broke from the Catholic Church because it would not grant him the divorce he desired

is where our story takes a tragic turn. As an example to any other religious houses who might attempt to resist the reforms, the monks of Lenton Priory met just about the bloodiest fate possible: they were publicly hanged, drawn and quartered. For these men of faith, their agonising deaths would have guaranteed them eternal salvation, and I can only hope they were able to hold onto this thought as they were dragged to meet their fates.

As an archaeologist, it is important to think carefully about how things end up in the ground. What happens to buildings when they are abandoned? What parts of the building and its contents are valuable enough to take away, and which might be left behind? The circumstances under which they were abandoned will have a huge impact upon this.

In the rare event of a natural disaster, such as the eruption of Mount Vesuvius in AD 79 that famously buried the Roman cities of Pompeii and Herculaneum, we might expect to find more surviving objects and buildings, as people were forced to abandon them relatively quickly and could not return. After the execution of Lenton Priory's monks, however, there would have been plenty of time for people to cannibalise the buildings. The stonework of the church, its glass windows, and lead window cames (the parts that hold the glass panes in place) would have been valuable enough to be taken away. Glass and lead can be re-melted and recycled into new objects, while stone can be reused in other buildings and frequently was throughout history.

Keep your eyes open and you will start to see this all over the place: circular millstones incorporated into the walls of buildings; parts of worked stone from churches found decorating people's gardens. The evidence for the past is knitted into the fabric of our world today if you only know to look for it. I had a pleasant surprise in Terri and Simon's

Old millstones, now incorporated into a wall

constructed from would have been stolen following the dissolution, we could still hope to find some clues to its layout in the building's foundations. For the construction of a large building such as a church, it is vital to dig deep foundation trenches into the earth at the base of the walls to support the weight of material above. While the decorative, above-ground masonry would have been a prime target for anybody taking apart the building to reuse its materials, the material filling the foundation trenches often survives in some form, and it is this that we hoped to find.

garden when I found a twisted fragment of lead window came that would originally have been moulded around the panes of the church's stained glass windows. Given that most of the lead from the church was probably recycled, this was a really special find and a good sign that there might be more evidence to come.

Even though much of the stone and other materials the priory church was

'You're not actually holding anything, Chloë'

Our perseverance was rewarded when we came upon what initially appeared to be a mound of stonework and rubble in one side of the trench. After some investigation, we were able to determine that we had found the remains of a wall foundation belonging to the priory church. We had found what we were looking for, and it was about to forever change our picture of how the church would have looked.

While the fancy facing of the walls was long ago robbed away to be reused elsewhere, our investigation uncovered the rubble infill and foundation cuts of a chapel added to the priory church in the 13th century

We had discovered the remains of a substantial piece of architecture. It was originally 'faced' with attractive worked stone and strengthened on the interior with rubble and mortar. It was probably the remains of a buttress, projecting from the apse of the church or out of a chapel connected to the apse. We know that monastic churches were remodelled in the 13th century to include smaller chapels attached to the main building. The location and orientation of these stones strongly suggested to us that we had the remains of an important chapel, known as a 'Lady Chapel' because it was dedicated to the Virgin Mary.

Digital Heritage expert Marcus Abbott was delighted with this new information as it provided vital clues for his reconstruction of the priory church. Looking at Marcus's reconstruction, I experienced a profound sense of the grandeur and prominence of Lenton Priory. It was a place of great

significance in the local area for hundreds of years, now a quietly unremarkable – albeit attractive – part of Nottingham. By working with experts such as Marcus, archaeology provides us with something akin to X-Ray goggles, through which we can flick through the many layers of time and reveal the ebb and flow in fortunes, meanings, and uses of a place.

The story of Lenton Priory didn't end there, though. Just as we thought we were wrapping up the dig, we had another surprise: the little trench in the students' garden had come down onto a medieval cobbled surface. We could tell based on its depth below ground that it was contemporary with the priory, and it was covered in fragments of pottery of the sort that ordinary people would have in their homes. Had we just uncovered evidence for ordinary people living far closer to the priory than we had previously thought?

Not all finds are ancient! Tash identifies a metal ring from some modern machinery in the top layers of the trench

One ring to rule them all

This cobbled surface shows how far below us the medieval ground surface was

Our time in Lenton taught us to expect the unexpected and helped us to rebuild the picture of how the priory church was modified and used over time. Although things ended tragically for the monks who were executed as traitors, the history of Lenton Priory was far deeper. We felt that we had managed to touch upon this and to help weave it into the story of the modern-day community, who now know of the magnificent and nationally important fragments of history that lie just a few feet beneath their houses, pubs and gardens.

Our work here allowed us to redraw the picture of Lenton's lost priory church

TROW POINT, SOUTH SHIELDS

Every so often on *The Great British Dig*, we do something a bit different, and step outside of people's back gardens to dig instead in larger community spaces. That was the case at the very special site of Trow Point, in South Shields. This windswept promontory looks out across the slate grey of the North Sea, and provides an excellent vantage point for the comings and goings at the mouth of the River Tyne.

It was its role as a vantage point that had brought us to this spot in the first place. Trow Point has seen intermittent use as a coastal defence site and military training area for over 150 years. Historical records mention the presence of defensive structures at the site as far back as the early 1800s, and the Victorians later built an experimental 'disappearing gun' here, a replica of which is present at the site today. The disappearing gun was a mechanical marvel that moved into a hidden position after firing, protecting the gunner while they reloaded. If you ever happen to visit the site, take note of the artificial mound on which the gun is mounted: this housed the pneumatic mechanism required to move the gun.

Unfortunately, the disappearing gun at Trow Point was not a successful experiment,

A replica of the Victorian 'disappearing gun' sits atop its original housing at Trow Point

as it took a whopping eight hours to return to a firing position! Personally, that makes it even more interesting to me. We often talk of technological innovations as though they are like switching on a lightbulb in the dark, but in reality, success is built upon failure, often multiple failures, and the gun at Trow Point was a fantastic example of this.

There was another reason behind us coming to Trow Point. Sadly, the archaeology is at risk due to coastal erosion. As my learned friend Don O'Meara explained to Hugh, we have perhaps 50 to 100 years before the whole cliff is lost to the sea. This meant that we chose to prioritise the spots closest to the cliff edge for excavation and recording. A fine idea, when you are planning the dig beforehand, but perhaps somewhat less attractive once you are standing there in the driving rain! Our time at Trow Point was a true endurance test, as we were determined not to let the wet and windy weather sabotage our efforts.

Archaeology makes us see the world differently. We knew that the various lumps and bumps across Trow Point were evidence for archaeological features. Unless land has been deliberately levelled (e.g. for ploughing), the locations of past ditches, collapsed buildings, burial mounds and anything else large and constructed by humans, remain visible in the landscape. If you ever visit the site of Grimes Graves in Norfolk, you will be met by an intensely cratered, almost lunar landscape. Each of the

Don O'Meara explains that within 100 years, the site at Trow Point will be lost to coastal erosion

400 pockmarks there represents the shaft of a mine, now largely – but not completely – filled in with soil. Those shafts were sunk over 5,000 years ago, in the British Neolithic, by people who wanted to acquire high quality flint to make stone tools.

We chose to excavate in four key locations across the promontory, answering questions about the nature of these features. This 'keyhole surgery' of the site would then be linked with a broader perspective, gained from what is known as an Earthworks survey, to be conducted by specialist Jim Brightman. Jim would be using a GPS to map out the

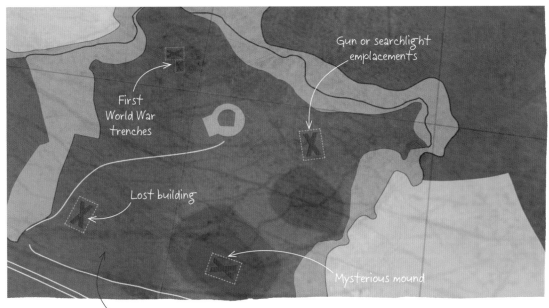

Gun or searchlight emplacements

First World War trenches

Lost building

Mysterious mound

Plan of Trow Point, with the location of our trenches marked 'X' topography of the site, which we would then be able to link with the evidence for chronology that can only come from digging. The GPS Jim was using is accurate to within 2cm, and all the data are fed into a computer that can map out with startling precision the undulations in the landscape.

Historical sources tell us that there were three main periods of military use of the site at Trow Point. First of all came the Third Durham Volunteers, who had a practice battery here in the 1860s. Later, when the First World War erupted in the summer of 1914, Trow Point became a training ground for the men of the Tyne Garrison before they headed out to the bloody battlefields of the Western Front. After the outbreak of the Second World War in 1939, the site returned to use as a genuine defensive position, but we didn't know much about how this would have looked, and it was one of the things we were hoping to investigate.

Richard and I were interested in two partially exposed concrete platforms, close to the cliff edge. They were clearly bases for something, but we weren't sure what: could they be coastal searchlights or artillery guns? Richard got to work, and rapidly uncovered both structures, just in time for a visit from retired Major Ian Jones, who served with the local 101st Artillery Regiment. Richard was able to identify these as gun emplacements, but there was more to the story, as Ian was about to reveal. He identified the emplacements as having been built in the late Victorian period, after the disappearing gun

Jim Brightman uses a highly accurate GPS to map the earthworks to within 2cm

was constructed. Two deep grooves in the platforms formed incomplete circles around the central pivots, allowing the guns to be rotated.

The partiality and location of these grooves meant they would only have been able to fire out directly into the sea, and not to be turned towards the mouth of the river. (The useful thing about Trow Point is that one can fire out into the sea without risk of hitting the marine traffic that would have busied the mouth of the Tyne.) This was a clue to their function: unlike the guns at nearby Tynemouth and Frenchman's Battery, they would have been built for artillery practice, rather than for defence. Richard seems to have lucked out on this occasion: he had solved the mystery of the emplacements by removing a single layer of soil and turf! We left him along with archaeologists Gulfareen and Frankie to record their findings.

Meanwhile, twin sisters Anne and Sheila were helping Tash to excavate an area that we hoped would reveal the remains of a lost building, known from historical maps. One of the wonderful things about community archaeology is that we are able to tap into the local knowledge, and memories, of the people we work with. The sisters explained to Tash that they played at Trow Point as children, at which point some of the building's remains – 'bricks and stuff' – were still visible above ground. Soon enough, various finds, including a door hinge, turned up, confirming our suspicions that some structural remains of the building would be found beneath.

'You're connected with the history of your land; of where you've come from,' remarked

Expert archaeologist Clare enjoyed being battered by the wind and sea so much that she moved to the Outer Hebrides

The partial grooves in these gun emplacements meant gunners could only have fired directly out to sea

Tash with twin sisters Anne and Sheila

I was particularly keen to investigate.

My instincts were on target this time around, as we soon found evidence for the feature cutting into the mound. We discovered a sharp change in soil type, which we were able to trace back to show the original size and shape of the cut. This is what we might describe as a 'connoisseur's trench', in that we were able to build a very interesting picture of what had happened here just by scrutinising the complex changes in the soil.

local volunteer Alan. We were certainly not short of hands on deck, in spite of the stormy weather. As well as various locals who were willing to brave the rain and wind, we were joined by Breaking Ground Heritage, an organisation that uses heritage and archaeology as a pathway to recovery for ex-servicemen and women. Former Royal Marine Dickie Bennett, who served in Afghanistan, explained that they had been attracted to working at the site by its military character.

Tash and I set the chaps working in a long trench that we had set up to investigate a mysterious mound. There was some speculation that this could be much older than the rest of the archaeology at Trow Point, as there was an old antiquarian record of a Bronze Age burial mound somewhere in the area. We also suspected that there was also a more recent feature that had been cut into the mound, indicated by a dip in the ground level, which

Perhaps more relatable to the non-connoisseur was a host of fantastic finds that came out of this part of the trench. Alan and I found several fragments of glass bottles with moulded lettering on them. This twentieth-century habit of visibly marking the location of manufacture is incredibly useful to the archaeologist, as you might imagine! We were able to identify one milk bottle fragment as

Dickie Bennet of Breaking Ground Heritage

Tash and I meet the volunteers from Breaking Ground Heritage

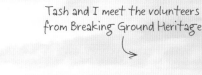

having come from Craven Dairies in Leeds, and another which came from Sunderland.

One particularly nice find from the upper levels here was a 10 pence piece dating to 1968, three years *before* the official switchover to decimalisation. This coin was among the new 5p and 10p coins that had been pre-minted in order to help people to get to grips with the new currency. I could imagine how strange it must have seemed at the time, when everybody was used to having 12 pennies to the shilling, and 20 shillings to the pound.

As we dug deeper, we started to get a picture of what this feature was. The shape and depth of the cut told us that we were probably standing in a weapons pit, a defensive foxhole for taking cover while firing at the enemy. Dating evidence arrived in the form of a spectacular find made by local volunteer Martin, albeit one that initially sparked caution in me. Martin had found what he thought was a bullet casing, but before handling it I had to check that it was spent. Happily, it was, and so we excitedly decided to take it over to Dig HQ, to garner the opinion of military historian Andy Robertshaw.

After carefully cleaning it up and examining its lettering under a microscope, Andy was able to tell us that what Martin had found was a .303 rifle cartridge, manufactured in 1943, in a munitions factory in Kidderminster. And it really was a good

We pieced together several fragments of this glass bottle, including the word 'Shields', suggesting local manufacture

We found several coins, including a very early 10p coin, and a ha'penny dating to 1908

job that it was spent, because as he explained to Hugh, this was a rare incendiary round, designed to set fire to things. We could now be confident that we were excavating a weapons pit dating to the Second World War, and this time we weren't looking at training activities. This was the real deal, part of the extensive coastal defence network designed to protect Britain from invasion.

Jim's earthworks survey was revealing a series of features right beside the cliff that had the dimensions and form of First World War trenches. Keen to investigate this hypothesis, we opened an archaeological trench cutting across one of them: a trench within a trench! I soon discovered that this was another connoisseur job, with complex archaeological layers suggesting that the features had been dug and re-dug multiple times.

A ha'penny (half penny) coin dating to 1908 confirmed that it likely belonged to the First World War features at the site, and – as I explained to Richard when he popped over for a visit – what we were finding was consistent with practice trenches, with the evidence for re-cutting confirming that they

Happily, this 1943 bullet was 'spent', meaning it had been fired and only the case remained

would have been constructed multiple times.

A War Grade bottle top dating to the 1940s provided an intriguing hint that they may even have been re-cut during the Second World War. Recognising a good bet, Richard decided to jump in and help, and began to uncover more and more evidence for the practice trenches. We found heavily corroded corrugated iron, which would have been used to shore up the sides of the trench, stains that told us where wooden structures had rotted away, but also some surviving fragments of wood.

Hugh brought Andy over from Dig HQ, so that he could help us to interpret the trench within a trench. Andy suspected that we were seeing evidence for practicing trench construction with different materials – wood, corrugated iron – so that the men would be prepared to use whatever was to hand when they arrived at the Front.

Having never had the opportunity to dig at any of the First World War battlefield sites in continental Europe, I was excited to have helped reveal a part of these practice trenches, which gave a real sense of the experience of the soldiers. Even better, we were now able to extrapolate this new knowledge out to the rest of the earthworks, showing that we were excavating a fire trench, with nearby communication trenches in a classic zigzagging pattern, a strategy employed on the Front to minimise the casualties when a shell hit. Keyhole surgery in action!

I met with Hugh and Don to discuss the relationship of the mound to the wider landscape, including the quarry

The weapons pit left a significant dip in the ground here

Back at the trench running over the mound, we were finally able to answer the question of whether it dated to the Bronze Age or not. While digging the weapons pit, we had spotted a layer of bricks and other materials from a building demolished in the late 19th or early 20th century. I wanted to know whether this demolition layer ran underneath the mound, because if it did, that would mean the mound had been constructed more recently, presumably at some point in the 20th century. To answer this question, we decided to take one section of the trench

First World War trench in Ypres, Belgium

a lot deeper. After digging through what seemed an endless layer of clay, I came down onto the same demolition material.

As much as it would have been nice to find a Bronze Age burial, I was pleased that we had been able to answer this particular

archaeological question. That's the thing about digging: just when you think you know what you're looking at, the archaeology throws you a curveball.

There was one last sting in the tail of this trench. Whilst I was drawing up the final plans along with fellow archaeologist Eleonora, a couple of local dog walkers popped by and cheerily informed us that the dip in the ground where the weapons pit had been was habitually used as a sort of unofficial toilet by certain members of the community. I still feel that I might have been happier without this *particular* piece of local knowledge.

As we neared the end of our time at Trow Point, Tash and her mini army of volunteers uncovered the story of what had happened to the house. A burnt demolition layer, filled with roof slate, lay over the preserved foundations of the house, including part of the chimney, and the porch. New dimensions were added to

The WWI practice trenches had been re-cut multiple times, and contained traces of corroded metal and wood

this story by Don, who analysed some of the burnt wood and found it to be pine, and Andy, who investigated the local census records. And it turns out that, like everything else we had found thus far at Trow Point, the house had military associations.

This was Trow Rock Gun Station, occupied at the time of the 1901 census by a Royal Artillery gunner named Charles Moore, and his wife, Margaret. Sometime between 1901 and the next census in 1911, the house was demilitarised and occupied by a civilian family, but it returned to the

military at the outbreak of war in 1914.

Not to let the history outdo the archaeology, however, the house provided us with one last, very special find. Tash had found a large fragment from a ceramic bottle, with some Russian script imprinted on it. As serendipity would have it, Tash is able to read Russian, and she identified the bottle as having come from a factory in Riga, Latvia, and having originally contained a strong alcohol. This factory was established in 1892, when Latvia was part of the Russian Empire, and the bottle of alcohol would have arrived

The complex zigzagging trenches constructed over 100 years ago are still visible in the surface undulations

in South Shields thanks to its trade links with the Baltic. Nonetheless, the bottle is not a typical find in the UK, so it is quite possible that it was brought here by a sailor from the region. A little piece of home.

Tash with her Latvian bottle

I felt profoundly moved, excavating that First World War practice trench at Trow Point. Many of the young men who originally trained here over a hundred years ago were never to return from what was known at the time as the Great War. There I was, re-revealing the trench they had dug, and looking out at the same cold, unforgiving North Sea. It was difficult not to feel sad at the loss of so many young lives, and the devastation that it wrought on a whole generation, but I also experienced a sense of connection, of hope. They may have died over a century ago but, through archaeology, we were able to reach out and touch their stories. To be human is to be eternal in that sense; we are all part of the same family, and the things we say and do can ring brightly forward, long after we ourselves are gone.

Coins

Coins are a wonderful, if somewhat lucky, find. This guide gives you a tiny glimpse into the enormous range of coins out there, but as ever, you will need to back it up with library and online research.

Note the characteristic edge that results from off-centre striking of the coin

Bronze sestertius of the Roman emperor Gordian III dating to AD 240

Late Iron Age and Roman coins

Coins arrived in Britain slightly before the Roman conquest. Parts of southern and eastern England had access to gold coins from the continent, often based upon Greek originals. In the 1st century BC, the first coins were minted in Britain itself. They were bronze, and featured Greek-style motifs.

From around 50 BC, coins in Britain started to be inscribed with the names of local rulers. Even before the Roman conquest of much of Britain a century later some Roman coins found their way here. Well-known Roman and Byzantine coins include the bronze sestertius, the silver denarius, and the gold solidus.

Recognising early coins

Most early coins were made by striking a blank piece of metal with an engraved die, although some were cast into a mould. If your coin has a stamped imprint with an often uneven fringe of unstamped metal around it, then it may well date to before the advent of mechanised coin manufacture in the late 17th century.

Medieval coins

After the Roman army left Britain, coin production became far less common, although scattered examples of imported coins exist, for example from the continuation of the Eastern Roman Empire in Byzantium. Along the east coast of England, you might be lucky enough to happen upon a small, silver sceat, which were minted from the 7th to the 9th century AD. The silver penny, first minted in Kent around AD 764, continued in use throughout England for centuries, and David I of Scotland introduced Scottish silver pennies in 1136.

It was during the medieval period that the majority of coins that you might have heard of were first minted, representing different denominations at different times; for example, shillings, crowns, ha'pennies and farthings. Indeed, the minting of new types or editions of coin were an important way

Silver sceattas of the 5th–6th century AD, found during excavations near Covent Garden in London

Gold coin dating to the reign of Edward III (1327–77). The denomination is a quarter-florin, also known as a half-leopard or Helm—medieval coin names can be confusing!

that medieval monarchs communicated ideas about how they wanted to be viewed by their subjects. All the kings and queens were depicted in slightly different ways, and working out which monarch you are looking at is often the first step to identifying what kind of coin you have found and how old it is.

Silver penny dating to the reign of Edward I (1239-1307)

These types of coin are known as 'long cross' pennies, named after the design where the cross on the reverse goes right to the edge

Coins show Edward I staring out at whoever's holding them

UK treasure laws

If you are lucky enough to find ancient or precious coins, make sure you report it in keeping with UK Treasure Laws. See page 148 for details.

Machine-made coins

From the later 17th century, coin production was mechanised for the first time. These new, so-called 'milled' coins can be recognised by their distinctive edges, which are far more regular than coins formed by striking with a die. They typically feature a series of ridges around them, designed to prevent the coins from being 'clipped' by counterfeiters who would shave the edges of coins to obtain the precious metals they were made from.

The decimalisation of British coins was introduced in 1971, although some decimal coins were pre-minted, as we discovered at Trow Point (Dig 4, see page 64). Even after decimalisation, there is much interest in the study of coinage and plenty of commemorative coins become collectors' items.

Queen Anne silver shilling, dating to 1707

Note the regular edge and ridged pattern to prevent clipping

HOT TIP! If you can make out the details on coins, they can help to date the other finds in a layer too. This is what archaeologists call a terminus post quem – the date after which the archaeological layer must have been laid down. For example, if we find a coin of Roman Emperor Septimius Severus, who reigned from AD 193 to 211, we know the layer can't have been present before at least AD 193.

20th-century coins, showing the reigning monarch at the time of issue

Date of issue

20th-century coins, showing the denominations and the date of issue

The incredibly long reign of Elizabeth II (her coronation was almost 70 years ago at the time of writing) has rendered us somewhat unused to seeing anything but her face on the front of our coins, but here you can see George VI (her father) and preceding monarchs Edward VII and George V.

Thanks to a combination of inflation and decimalization, coin denominations such as 'half penny' (or ha'penny) and 'three pence' (or thruppence / thruppenny bit) are no longer in currency, and make fantastic collectors' items

DIGGING LEGALLY AND SAFELY

With your background research done and your tools gathered, it's very tempting to just get stuck in, but there are some important things to think about before starting the excavation.

AT A GLANCE

- ☐ Get landowner permission
- ☐ Check scheduled monuments list
- ☐ Wear safe boots
- ☐ Look out for hazardous materials
- ☐ Keep tools tidy
- ☐ Don't stand on the trench edge
- ☐ Don't dig too deep
- ☐ Step the trench if you need to

THE LEGAL BIT

Some archaeological sites have legal protection as scheduled monuments, which means that you can't dig within their boundaries without written permission from whichever government body oversees heritage and archaeology in the different parts of the United Kingdom. A quick internet search for the region you live in plus the term 'scheduled monuments' should throw up the correct webpages straight away.

Wales: Cadw
Scotland:
    Historic Environment Scotland
Northern Ireland:
    Department for Communities
England:
    Historic England

The bodies that oversee scheduled monuments in the different countries of the United Kingdom

Lle
Porth-Daear i Gymru

Henebion Cofrestrig

Cadw

Crynodeb   Rhagolwg   Diweddbwyntiau (2)   Lawrlwythiadau (4)   Metadata (4)

View in Lle Map Browser cy

There are some other ways that land can be protected in law, unrelated to heritage or archaeology. For example, special permission is also needed to dig in Sites of Special Scientific Interest (SSSIs). If you are unsure, then it is always worth checking with the relevant government body for the country in which you're working (Defra, Scottish Natural Heritage, Natural Resources Wales and DAERA in Northern Ireland).

Naturally, if you are hoping to dig on somebody else's land, you will need permission from the landowner before you start. Even if you're on friendly terms with them, it's probably best to get this in writing, either on paper or via email.

SAFE AND COMFORTABLE DIGGING

Some digging tools are sharp, some are heavy and some are both! It is really important that you use digging tools carefully, always making sure you are aware of anyone close by. When working on an archaeological site, most archaeologists wear safety boots with steel toecaps and midsoles to guard against accidents with mattocks and spades.

When using spades and shovels, ensure that you keep your back straight and bend your knees to avoid injury. If you're not used to this, take some time to practise it, as it will save you

Like our Tash herself, her workwear is fun on the outside, but made of steel on the inside – steel toe-capped work boots

Gloves can prevent blisters

untold pain later on. While you are shovelling spoil out of the ground, it's better not to overload your tool, and to maintain a nice steady rhythm. You might also wish to invest in some gardening gloves to help prevent blisters, and a little kneeling mat or knee pads. Professional archaeologists will tell you that not doing these things will only shorten your digging career!

KEEPING YOUR SITE TIDY

It can be tempting to leave a lot of tools, nails and bits of string lying around within easy reach of your trench. Always putting tools away after you've used them or stacking things neatly a short distance from the trench means that you and others are less likely to trip or stumble. Especially if your trench is starting to get a little deep, this can be really important in preventing nasty accidents. Be particularly careful about where you lay the larger tools: nobody wants to experience that classic slapstick moment of stepping on a hoe and having the shaft ping up and hit them in the face!

DON'T LIVE ON THE EDGE

On a related note, make sure that everybody in your household is aware of the golden rule: never stand with your feet edging over the trench edge! Dear reader, you would not believe the number of times I have had to remind our lovely TV crew of this rule, and even at times, one or two of our senior archaeologists.

Richard respecting the edge of his trench by maintaining a little distance between it and his feet

The edge of the trench is its most fragile point, and it could easily collapse. This is bad for the archaeology, but it is potentially lethal for anybody who is in the trench when it happens. If you have seen the movie The Dig, you may recall the moment when everybody is scrabbling to free archaeologist Basil Brown from under a collapsed mound of soil. Health and safety regulations may be great fodder for observational comedy, but there are multiple real examples of archaeologists and workers being buried alive before we became so strict about them.

SPOTTING UNSAFE MATERIALS

Quite often, you might find that the upper layers of a trench include the debris of more recent demolished buildings. If these buildings had asbestos roofing or insulation and it has not been properly disposed of, there is a chance you'll encounter it. Asbestos is extremely dangerous when broken, so you need to know how to spot it. Some common types are illustrated here, but there are many more and it comes in a range of colours, so if you find anything at all that you're unsure about, the first thing to do is an internet image search. If you do encounter asbestos, it must be disposed of by a professional, licensed specialist.

NOT DIGGING TOO DEEP

It can be hard to resist digging a little bit deeper, trying to find just a little bit more. One of the most potentially dangerous aspects of archaeology, however, is the risk of collapse as mentioned before. Most trenches, particularly those in gardens, are likely to be small and fairly shallow, so the risk is minimal.

There is no single universal rule for what depth makes a trench 'unsafe' as it depends on what you are digging through. Clay, for example, is much more stable than a sandy soil or loose rubble. A lot of archaeologists would consider stepping out their trench at around 1m deep, by decreasing the size of the area being excavated, leaving a step of 30cm or more in width on one of the sides.

Regardless of whether you choose to step your trench, you must keep a regular check on its sides for any areas that seem loose or crumbly. Your safety is always more important than exploring archaeological remains, and the golden rule is that if you feel uncomfortable with what your trench sides look like, then stop!

Corrugated asbestos

Asbestos pipe

Asbestos insulation

DIG 5 FROM MILL TO POW CAMP

OLDHAM, GREATER MANCHESTER

We met Hugh at the site of a disused Second World War pillbox in Oldham, Greater Manchester, in the hope of finding evidence for a Prisoner of War (POW) camp that had been set up in a former cotton mill.

This massive, five-storey cotton spinning mill was built in 1903 and remained in operation until 1938. We wanted to know how and why the mill had been adapted to host its prisoners and to find evidence for their daily lives and experiences. Up to 6,000 men would have been housed here at Glen Mill, some of whom stayed until its closure in 1947. We know from historical records that the prisoners were mostly German and Italian,

but some Russians were also sent here.

As we were primarily looking for evidence dating to the mill's use as a POW camp, we were lucky enough to be joined once more by military historian Andy Robertshaw. Andy was excited about the opportunity to dig here as the vast majority of POW camps were demolished soon after the war, along with all their secrets. As he told Hugh,

Oldham, Greater Manchester, was made world-famous by its cotton mills

Marching forwards to investigate Glen Mill POW Camp

Local residents Leah and Ross

the mill would have undergone a massive conversion process when it was co-opted in 1939. There would have been sleeping quarters, a hospital, a kitchen and a recreational area to allow the men to exercise in the open air. The site would also require security features, of course, to stop the POWs from escaping.

I joined local resident Marissa and two of her children in their front garden where we were digging a 1 x 1m test pit with the help of professional archaeologist Ayesha. While most of the gardens in which we were digging were located over the remains of the mill, historical maps suggested that Marissa's garden lay over a mysterious outbuilding, the function of which we were keen to discover. Could it be the living quarters of the mill manager, or was it something to do with POW camp?

Ayesha and I soon discovered that this was going to be a difficult site to dig. The ground was almost rock-solid, so even de-turfing was rather more difficult than usual. We were determined to persevere, though! Marissa had told me that she always wanted to be an archaeologist as a child, so I was determined for us to help her realise that dream, even if just a little. Her twin children

Marissa had always loved the idea of doing archaeology, while her twins hoped to find rubies!

Shan and Safira were keen on helping out too, and they were soon trowelling away in the little test pit. The family had told me they'd like to find bones or perhaps – on Shan's request – some diamonds, but one of the first finds from this trench was rather more humble and closer to the kids' experiences: a plastic toy building block. Bricks were certainly on our list of things we hoped to find, although we had been expecting somewhat larger ones!

One of the loveliest moments of the season was when Hugh and Richard knocked on a door and discovered that the occupants of the house, Ben and Becky, were already huge fans of the show. It turns out that the whole family were really interested in archaeology and history, and they immediately leapt at the opportunity of us invading their garden. Even more excitingly, they had existing family links to the POW camp as Becky's great-grandfather had worked there. Their garden lay over what we believed to be the back wall and rear rooms of the mill complex, which would have housed the boiler room. We hoped to find some evidence for the construction of the mill's walls and perhaps some clues as to what was going on in the narrow space between the boundary fencing and the POW camp buildings.

Unfortunately, the first few days in Oldham were really tough for everybody involved in digging. A fragment of medieval pottery found early on had got us all rather excited, but we were soon to realise that it had come from a thick layer of material that had been imported to cover the site after the mill's demolition. Furthermore, this layer was a dense, clayey soil that really demanded a lot of effort to remove, and morale was getting low. Everybody was starting to worry that we weren't going to find any archaeology here at all.

Until the later 20th century, the destruction of existing buildings to make way for new ones would leave clear archaeological traces in the form of demolition layers, surviving foundations, and other features that were too deep for destruction or that were redeposited in the same location during levelling of the site. The scale of

Richard and Hugh knocking on Ben and Becky's door. Turns out, the family were already fans of the show...

COTTONOPOLIS

Although there are many stages to making textiles, the key processes are converting the plant or animal fibre into yarn (thread) by spinning it, and then weaving these threads together to create a fabric. Various methods of spinning and weaving have been practised over time, but it was the mechanisation of these processes in the 18th century that allowed textile production to take place on an industrial scale. Manchester's first cotton mill dates to 1783 and was water-powered, adapting the ancient technology of the water wheel to power a series of clever recent inventions that mechanised various aspects of textile manufacture.

A key moment was the development of a steam engine that could reliably drive a cotton mill in 1785. Suddenly, it was possible to build a cotton mill anywhere – not just on a watercourse – and power it via boilers that produced as much as was required of the necessary steam. The first steam-powered mill in Manchester was the Piccadilly Mill, opened in 1789, but by 1800 there were over 40 of them.

People flooded to the city from all over rural Britain and Ireland, desperate to find work in the factories as traditional craft industries waned.

Dubbed 'Cottonopolis', the influx of workers meant that Manchester was thrust into a rapid and unplanned process of urbanisation, and many people found themselves both living and working in unhealthy and unpleasant circumstances. Child labour was rife in the mills, and because of these dire social circumstances, the city became a hub not only of industry and

ABOVE A young boy mule spinning at Jones's Cotton Mill, Manchester, 1909

LEFT Manchester in the late 19th century – a city built on mills

OPPOSITE Shop for mill hands set up during the 'cotton famine' at Mr Birley's Mill, Manchester, 1862

capitalism, but of social revolution.

Manchester's situation at this time was hugely influential upon world politics. German philosopher and economist Friedrich Engels travelled to Manchester for clerical work, aged 22. Here, he met an Irish radical named Mary Burns, a factory worker. The pair sustained a monogamous relationship until her death 20 years later though they never married, deeming the institution a form of class oppression. Burns helped to guide his research, showing him the worst of the Manchester slums and the horrors of industrial accidents and child labour. In 1845 he published *The Condition of the Working Class in England*, in which he argued that the grim conditions in Manchester were the logical outcome of capitalism and industrialisation. Three years later, in 1848 and having travelled back to Germany, Engels co-authored the *Communist Manifesto* with Karl Marx.

Unfortunately, the cotton industry was bound up with human misery in more ways than one because much of the raw cotton worked in

Manchester's mills was imported from the slave plantations of the American South. This meant that during the American Civil War of 1861–5, imports of raw cotton decreased and its price rose. Because there had previously been such a boom in production, mill owners suddenly found themselves with too much fabric to sell and not enough money to buy the raw cotton required to make more. They greatly decreased their production and many cotton workers lost

their jobs. The so-called 'cotton famine' ensued, with the sudden unemployment of vast numbers of people across the north west of England. Soup kitchens were set up, and classes to help train workers in other skills were organised by local churches.

The lot of the textile workers was eventually to improve, however, as the industry reinvigorated itself following the end of the American Civil War. An extraordinary 145 cotton mills were built in Oldham between 1873 and 1875 alone, which became one of the spinning capitals of the world. Even as late as 1913, Manchester processed 65% of the world's cotton. It was not to last forever, of course. During the First World War, the British government began to establish mills in South Asia, exporting the spinning technology and very often the re-purposed machinery itself. The Great Depression caused by the Wall Street Crash in 1929 compounded this blow, with a profound and long-lasting impact upon the region.

The machine-made Glossop brick

modern construction, however, means that entire archaeological sites, with all the layers of history they contain, are vulnerable to complete erasure. This is why we have policies in place to protect the most important and vulnerable archaeology, such as cemeteries or sites of historical importance, by ensuring that they are recorded by professional archaeologists before the construction takes place.

Certain monuments are deemed so important that they are 'scheduled' – legally protected due to their historical value. You need written permission from your regional Historic England office to carry out archaeological or construction work at a scheduled monument, and the reasons for doing so would have to be good! The site of Glen Mill, of course, was not deemed important enough to be covered by these

laws, and the developers built here entirely legally and responsibly. But the level of destruction was a stark reminder of what might happen to our archaeology if the existing protections are relaxed too far.

All was not yet lost, however, and we began to turn up some interesting finds. As we had hoped, we started to find some bricks, included stamped bricks and a handmade brick that was older than the mill itself. Keen to chat bricks, finds specialist Dr David Griffiths bumped brains with industrial archaeologist Ian Miller, who has a most appropriate surname, as he was here to help us piece together the longer history of the mill before it was converted into a POW camp. One of Richard's bricks was stamped with the word 'Glossop' and almost certainly came from the original mill itself, a rare surviving fragment of the building.

As we continued to dig, Hugh and Andy made a great

Dr David Griffiths lends us his bricks-pertise

escape to walk around the periphery of the original mill and POW camp. A portion of the camp's original fencing survives to this day, the barbed wire providing a startling reminder of the bleak history of the site. Andy explained that originally, there was also a second fence, known as a 'kill fence' because anybody going beyond it would be shot by the guards. Although escape was difficult, it did happen. Documentary evidence exists for the successful escape of two German prisoners who made it back to Hamburg and sent the camp commandant a letter saying 'won't be returning for your hospitality'. Prisoners really did try to escape by digging secret tunnels, and one measure to prevent them from doing so was to sew circular patches on their uniforms, over neatly cut holes.

Parts of the POW outer fence still survive in the area to this day

Distinctive patches on POW uniforms would make escape more difficult

To research the area, Hugh visits a surviving mill with social historian Dr Michala Hulme, and the local archives with me

We found a rare surviving plan of the mill's conversion to a POW camp

Andy turned up some historical photographs of the prisoners

Could these belt buckles have belonged to a POW?

drawn up in advance of its conversion to a POW camp. What had originally been the scutching room, where seeds were removed from the cotton, was converted into a mess room where the men would have eaten and recreational activities would have taken place. The drainage system had to be substantially altered too, so that it ran from the mess room and all the way to the front of the mill building. This would surely have provided some temptation to those

This way, even if they removed the patches, the holes would give them away as escaped POWs to anybody they encountered.

Hugh also teamed up with me to pay a special trip to Oldham's historical archives to find out whether we could get our hands on any records of how the mill was converted into a camp. Happily, we discovered that the archive was jam-packed with maps and plans. We even discovered some of the original plans of the mill, with its various different rooms marked. Even better, we were able to compare these with the Ministry of Defence plans that were

Industrial archaeology expert Ian Miller examines a fragment of the mill's economiser, an innovative fuel-saving device

A fragment of painted floor from the camp hospital

prisoners who were determined to tunnel their way to escape!

All the hard work Richard was doing in Ben and Becky's garden finally paid off when they found some buckles that would have been used to hold up a set of trouser braces, and an early 20th-century coin. Meanwhile, Tash was also making some interesting

archaeological discoveries as she found a fragment of what would have been the floor of the POW camp's hospital.

More documentary evidence was also gathered by Andy, who showed Hugh something extremely interesting that provided a genuine insight into the daily life of the POW camp. It turns out that Friedrich

Histories entangled: Becky's great-grandfather worked at the POW camp

Humorous watercolours of life at Glen Mill, by ex-POW Friedrich Frauböse

Frühmorgens wenn noch alle pennen, die Eimer langsam überschwemmen.

"While most of us are sleeping still, the buckets start to overspill"

Characteristic patches on the POW uniforms

Frauböse, a German imprisoned in the camp, had painted several watercolour images detailing its daily life. One image showed that Friedrich slept in the main mill building, while another depicted the prisoners putting on a theatre performance. Yet more wonderful paintings depicted prisoners working in the vegetable gardens, kitchens and grounds, taking a medical exam, and picking up cigarette butts from the yard.

Taken together the evidence we had unearthed from people's back gardens and the local historical archives provided much food for thought. Many of the men imprisoned here would have been young, in their late teens and early twenties. Not all of them would have been willing soldiers. How had their time at a British POW camp affected them, and did they put it from their minds forevermore, or stop to think of it in later years?

'Hugh, can I get out now? Hugh? Anybody?'

Porcelain and its imitations

Porcelain, also referred to as china, is a ceramic material made of specially selected clays and fired to an extremely high temperature, resulting in a delicate, glassy, slightly translucent product that has been much sought after over the centuries.

The art of making and decorating porcelain stems from East Asia, and particularly China (hence the name), a development of glazing techniques from the Islamic world. White porcelain was decorated by hand with blue pigment and coated in transparent glaze, resulting in intricate and exquisite designs.

Ming Dynasty jar, early 16th century China

Thanks to long-distance trade between East Asia and the lands to its west along what is commonly known as the Silk Road, porcelain became increasingly popular in Europe from the later 16th century. The secrets to making it were jealously guarded, but potters tried to copy it anyway, spawning a range of 'blue and white' wares. Some of these, such as Dutch Delftware, were so sophisticated they became sought-after in their own right.

Chinese porcelain appears in 16th century paintings

18th-century Delftware, made in the Netherlands

The key to true porcelain is that the clay is fired to such a high temperature that it becomes slightly glassy – technically known as vitrification. In their quest to discover the secrets of creating the appearance of porcelain, craftspeople adapted what they already knew about glazing ceramics to try to imitate as best they could the finished appearance of porcelain. Many imitations were impressive and beautiful in their own right, but they give themselves away in the break.

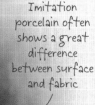

Imitation porcelain often shows a great difference between surface and fabric

True porcelain is glassy, and slightly translucent at the edges

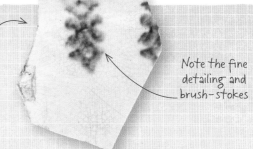

Hand-painted porcelain was the most time-consuming, and thus expensive

Note the fine detailing and brush-strokes

Spongeware, a blue and white pottery

The slightly random and naturalistic appearance of this decoration tell us it was applied by sponge

True porcelain

If you examine a broken fragment of porcelain pottery, you will see that even the inner part of the pot is almost glass-like in its smoothness and uniformity. If you hold them up to the light, the thinner edges are semi-transparent.

Imitation blue and white pottery

In imitations, the shiny surface contrasts with the rougher fabric of the pot beneath.

Transfer-printed blue on white pottery

Printed pottery usually has sharper and more intricate designs

Blue and white decoration techniques

In addition to determining whether a fragment is porcelain or one of its imitations, you can also work out what techniques were used to decorate it.

Hand-painted wares were the earliest and the most costly to produce, but other techniques such as sponging the pigment on and mass production using transfers eventually developed. The majority of these ceramics are white and decorated in blue, but there are also various multi-colour designs to look out for!

Note the difference between the white, glassy surface, and the darker fabric in the break

THE FINAL FRONTIER

DIG 6

FALKIRK, STIRLINGSHIRE

The legacy of the Roman Empire is so staggeringly important to us that it feels immediate and present to this day, over 2,000 years after it began. People continue to learn Latin and Ancient Greek, the main languages of the empire, its might is constantly revisited in film and television dramas, and Roman law even lies at the basis of our present-day legal system.

With Richard unable to join us as he was working elsewhere that week, Tash and I met Hugh in Falkirk, central Scotland, to investigate a unique point in history in which the might of the Roman Empire was pitched against the resilience of the Caledonians on its most northerly frontier.

By the 2nd century AD, most of England and Wales had been conquered, or at least subdued, by the Roman army, and the frontiers were heavily guarded against those people to the north who had thus far managed to resist. During the reign of the Emperor Hadrian, there was a consolidation

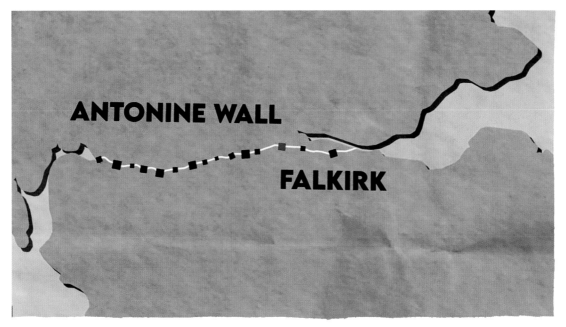

of the frontier in northern England, including the construction of the wall that bears his name to this day. Hadrian's successor, Antoninus Pius, aimed to make his mark by further extending the reach of empire. Under his rule, the Roman army again conquered the resistant lands to the north of Hadrian's Wall, entering what is now southern Scotland. In AD 142 the construction of what came to be known as the Antonine Wall began.

It was a formidable barrier, at 3m high and 5m wide, and stretched across the isthmus (narrow strip of land) between the Firth of Forth and the Firth of Clyde, marking for posterity what was to become the most northerly frontier ever achieved by the Roman Empire.

This much we know thanks to historical sources, but although they give us an overview of the movements of the Roman army, they are lacking in detail. Enter the archaeologists! As Tash and I explained to Hugh, the area surrounding the town of Falkirk had already seen some archaeological intervention, and local archaeologists had conjectured the probable line of the wall, and the size and location of the fort. To date, however, nobody had excavated *within* the location of the fort itself at Falkirk. We hoped that by opening trenches in the gardens of willing local residents, we could shed light on the internal layout, and pin down the size and precise location of Falkirk's fort.

We also wanted to catch some glimpses of the daily lives of the soldiers who had lived

THE FALKIRK FORT

Near this spot in the Pleasance area stood the Roman fort of Falkirk, part of the defensive system associated with the great 38 mile Antonine Wall constructed around 142 AD. It ran across Central Scotland from Dumbarton in the west to Bo'ness in the east. The Wall was inscribed in July 2008 as a World Heritage Site becoming part of the Frontiers of the Roman Empire World Heritage Site along with Hadrian's Wall. The Wall itself and its huge V shaped ditch crossed the town from Callendar Park in the east to Watling Lodge, Camelon in the west, and over the centuries a great deal of evidence for its location has been uncovered by archaeologists. The location of the fort was confirmed in 1992 when a team from Falkirk Museums excavated the site where the Scout Hall stands. There was some evidence of a pre-Roman settlement as well as extensive ditching from the Antonine period. There were also the remains of kilns, charcoal and iron slag suggesting the likelihood of an annexe used for semi-industrial activities attached to the fort.

Most of the Antonine
Wall was built of turf

here so many years ago. We certainly had our work cut out for us. The Roman army was nothing if not efficient, and its troops made careful use of whatever materials were locally available when constructing their defensive features. While much of Hadrian's Wall to the south was made of stone, the Antonine Wall and the outer defences of its forts were built from high stacks of turf, which would be visible only by characteristic changes in the buried soil.

One thing that makes this wall so valuable to archaeologists is that its occupation was relatively brief. The Caledonians, it turns out, were not that easy to subdue, and the frontier was abandoned by AD 162, its troops retreating to reoccupy Hadrian's Wall to the

south. As we discovered in Dig 1 at Benwell, the archaeology of Hadrian's Wall requires the careful unpicking of the changes and redevelopment stemming from centuries of occupation, and early phases were often destroyed by later rebuilding. The Antonine Wall, by contrast, offers a sort of time capsule: a snapshot of the expansion of the Roman Empire in the 2nd century AD. As for Antoninus Pius himself, he did not live to see the defeat of his new frontier, having died the previous year.

While Tash headed off to dig in people's gardens, I set to work alongside highly experienced archaeologist Robin, opening a long trench in the patch of grass belonging to the local Girl Guides' hut. Based on the previous projections, this trench should have been just inside the fort, with the Antonine Wall immediately to its north, and by digging here, we hoped to find evidence for the road that would have led in and out of the fort on its defended frontier.

Almost immediately, Robin and I discovered some really interesting – albeit unexpected – finds in our trench: a fragment of a large ink bottle and a slate pencil, both dating to the 19th century. The ink bottle was just the sort a teacher might have had on their desk, and Robin's trusty historical Ordnance Survey map of the area showed us that there had been a charity school nearby at the time. The teacher would have used their ink bottle to fill the smaller inkwells in the children's desks, but most of the time they would have written on slate, which was far

cheaper as it could be wiped clean and reused – hence the slate pencil. For the Guides and Brownies, these objects provided a direct glimpse into the experience of the charity school pupils in this area over 150 years ago and got them thinking not only about how different their lives must have been, but of all

We hoped that these gardens would yield evidence for what was happening in the Roman territory south of the fort

An inkwell in the Girl Guides' hut may have belonged to a 19th-century charity school

the things they would have had in common.

Tash was chatting with local homeowners Brent and Heather about what we hoped to find in their garden. Although he is a full-time lawyer, in his spare time Brent is an eager amateur historian and has spent years teasing Heather and their son with the thought that he would one day dig up the garden to look for Roman finds. Naturally

enough, he was delighted when a team of archaeologists offered to do the job for him!

We opened this test pit, along with two more in nearby gardens, in the hope of catching some glimpses of what was going on to the south of the fort. Would we find part of the Roman road that led south from the frontier? Or perhaps evidence for the defences surrounding the fort wall, such as

Tash found a copper token known as a jeton

the so-called 'ankle-breaker' ditches, which earned their name due to a nasty little slot at the base, designed to trip up any would-be attackers? As in the Guide Hut, evidence for the Romans had remained elusive thus far, but we could see this area was clearly rich in the archaeology of subsequent periods, as shown by a beautiful little medieval 'jeton' – a token that could be used in counting and trade – that popped out of Brent and Heather's trench.

I'm going to let you in on a secret. Archaeologists will always tell you that not finding what you are looking for is just as valuable as finding it, because the key thing is that it answers an archaeological question – but the truth is that we are in this job because we *love* finding things. Structures, objects, even stains in the ground that tell us something about what was there before – these are an archaeologist's bread and butter.

I was becoming increasingly frustrated, therefore, with the lack of Roman finds in Trench 1. Several layers deep, and we were

encountering plenty of archaeology but not the slightest evidence for Romans. I headed up to Dig HQ to chat with digital heritage expert and archaeologist Marcus Abbott, hoping that he could shed some light on why Trench 1 was not behaving herself.

As it turns out, Marcus had also been scratching his head over the location of the wall. He was trying to marry up the aerial data and the projected location of the wall and fort, but something wasn't adding up. As he sagely pointed out, Roman engineers were well-practised at adapting themselves to the lie of the land, and given that there was a natural ridge here, it would have been odd to locate the defensive wall itself lower down, as previous projections had done. The difference between these projections and Marcus's idea was only a matter of 5m or so but was crucial to our investigations, because if he was correct, Trench 1 lay *outside* the fort,

101

and north of the Antonine Wall. We couldn't be sure yet, but this would certainly explain the complete lack of Roman finds.

Armed with this new idea, but not quite sure how to break it to Robin, I returned to the garden of the Girl Guides' Hut to ponder the best course of action. Perhaps sensing that more heavy digging might be in the offing on site, Hugh had disappeared to do some investigation of his own. He met the University of Glasgow's Dr Louisa Campbell at the site of Rough Castle, the best-preserved fort on the Antonine Wall. Louisa explained that at the time of its construction this was the most fortified wall in the entire Roman Empire, and it cut right through the middle of a cultural landscape. The wall would have instantly carved a division between the people living on either side of it, who until that point shared language, culture, and social ties. Like an ancient equivalent of the Berlin Wall, these unlucky Caledonians saw their fates determined and their lives

divided by an enormous, external power.

Louisa also took Hugh to examine some surviving defensive pits, known as *lilia*. Only found to date at the site of Rough Castle, each of these pits would have had a sharpened wooden stake in the middle, ready to impale the unhappy enemy. She explained that although Roman forts were built to a broadly similar plan, there was also room for adapting this model to suit the circumstances. For example, at Rough Castle, the Commander's House had been located to the left, rather than the right of HQ as was the norm, but nothing was yet known about the size or internal layout at Falkirk Fort. It seemed there was a lot riding on this, and we were going to have to start finding some evidence for Roman Falkirk soon.

Hope soon appeared in the form of some Roman pottery, found by Don in a soil

Hugh visits Dr Louisa Campbell at the Rough Castle, another fort along the Antonine Wall

sample he took from Trench 2. Not to be outdone, Tash rapidly unearthed some more pottery, and this was the good stuff! She had found a beautiful fragment of what is commonly known as 'Samian ware', an attractive and relatively high-status Roman pottery type featuring moulded decoration and a shiny red finish.

Tash was then called to one of her other garden trenches, which was slotted tightly in the narrow space between the house and a flowerbed. Also wedged into this space were archaeological legend David 'The Badger' Connolly, and exuberant local resident Stuart. Stuart is in possession of a vast collection of custom-made Hawaiian shirts, which he sports while cycling around the streets of Falkirk. All

agreed that finding Roman pottery was a good sign, but if we were to answer the burning questions we came here with, we urgently needed evidence for some of the building structures associated with the fort.

I had made up my mind. I met with Hugh and Tash to discuss strategies, and we agreed

The remains of defensive pits known as *lilia* at Rough Castle

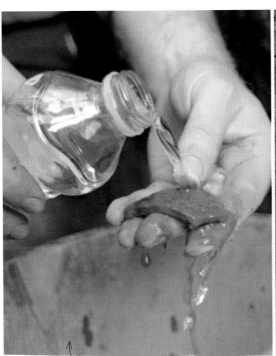

Don finds Roman pottery in Tash's trench

that although we had very little time left, our unsuccessful attempt to find the Romans in the Guide Hut garden had left too many open questions. Taking into account the time needed for recording and backfilling, I had just one day in which to dig a second, smaller test pit at the southern end of the garden. If Marcus was correct, then I should find evidence for either the wall itself or the interior layout of the fort. And if he wasn't, well, let's just say he'd owe me a pint or two for my troubles.

Tash, meanwhile, was putting all of her hopes into the trench she was digging with Stuart and the Badger, as her others had turned up some lovely medieval finds and very little else. It was a critical moment, so Tash and I kept the conversation brief, desperate to roll up our sleeves and go back to digging.

Naturally enough, at the mention of yet more heavy digging, Hugh trotted off to visit the remains of yet another Roman fort,

this time in Bearsden, East Dunbartonshire. Here, he met up with Dr Lindsay Allason-Jones, a leading expert in Roman archaeology with an illustrious career behind her, and a person close to my own heart as, like me, she had worked for many years as a lecturer at Newcastle University. Lindsay showed Hugh the surviving latrines and bathhouse that had once served this fort. For the Romans, a visit to the baths was as much about socialising as hygiene, and it was a complex operation.

The bathhouse at Bearsden featured seven different rooms including steam rooms, hot and cold baths, and a dry room. Although the main bathhouses would have been located outside the forts for safety reasons (heating them required constant stoking of fires!), Lindsay pointed out that the commanding officer would most likely have had his own private bathhouse attached to his residence within the fort itself. She also treated Hugh to a little tour of a slightly less savoury, but nonetheless crucial, part of Roman fort life: the latrines.

Tash finds a fragment of Samian Ware

Hugh meets Lindsay Allason-Jones at Bearsden bathhouse

Tash was making some extraordinary discoveries in the lower levels of her trench. First up was a fragment of what appeared to be a flue tile, an essential part of Roman heating systems and some pretty strong evidence for the presence a bathhouse. Given the earlier finding of fancy pottery, could Tash and David have been digging in the vicinity of the Commander's House?

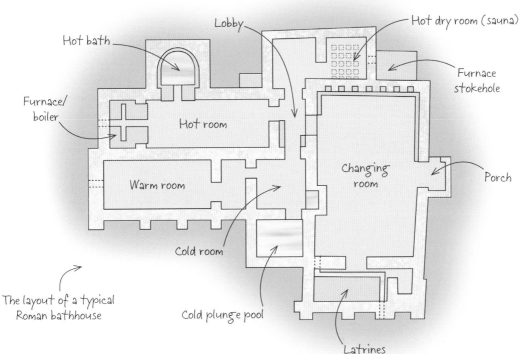

Hot bath

Lobby

Hot dry room (sauna)

Furnace/boiler

Hot room

Furnace stokehole

Warm room

Changing room

Porch

Cold room

Cold plunge pool

The layout of a typical Roman bathhouse

Latrines

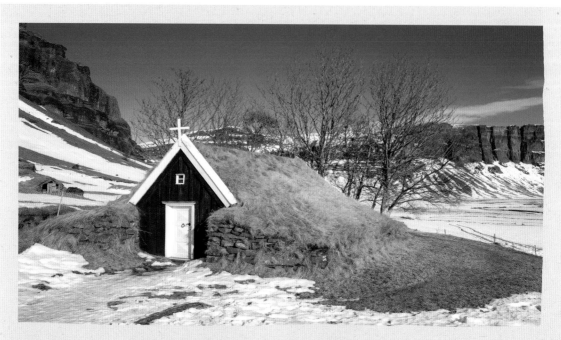

BUILDING WITH TURF

We spend plenty of time removing turf to get to the archaeology on *The Great British Dig*, but this time we had encountered ancient turf, buried beneath the layers of archaeology that had built up here over time. Turf actually makes a fantastic building material, so it's no surprise the Romans made use of it, but identifying it takes a slightly more trained eye than tracing the remains of their stone buildings.

Buried turf walls can be identified by variations in the colour and make-up of the soil, depending upon how the turf was stacked. This is because the upper part of each turf is richer in organic materials, whereas the lower part is richer in minerals (see Practical 5: All About Soil, page 130). When turf is buried or stacked, the usual soil processes are frozen, and the difference between these layers becomes more pronounced, with

characteristic patterns depending on how the turf was stacked (grass to grass, diagonally, etc.). For example, iron minerals often lend a more reddish tinge to the soil, so where turfs in an iron-rich soil have been stacked directly above one another, you would see reddish layers alternating with darker ones.

The ancient tradition of building with turf continued through the medieval period and beyond in many parts of northern Europe, for the simple reason that where locally available it is effective, economical, and efficient. It is excellent at insulating the inside of buildings from the cold, while the entangled roots system help to consolidate and bind together the different layers of building material. Should you be lucky enough to visit Iceland, you can visit fine examples of surviving turf-buildings. Sadly, few people alive today are trained in building with turf, and so we risk losing much

of our knowledge of this sustainable building technique.

From excavations elsewhere along the line of the Antonine Wall, we know that the Roman soldiers building it first laid a 4m wide stone foundation. This would have provided stability and helped with drainage, making the wall less susceptible to rot or to freezing damage. Having laid the foundations, they would then have gone ahead with cutting and building up the turfs on top, to a height of about 3m. That is approximately 20 layers of turf, topped with a wooden walkway. Rather wonderfully, an iron turf cutter – not unlike those we use today while opening our trenches on people's lawns – was found by archaeologists at the Roman Fort at Newstead in Roxburghshire.

Their hard work was further rewarded as they finally discovered evidence for structure. They carefully revealed a set of characteristic patterns in the soil: the remains of a turf wall. This must have been part of the large turf wall that surrounded the fort itself, but finding it here was a huge surprise. It was telling us that Falkirk Fort was smaller than had originally been thought, and would likely have been garrisoned by only half a cohort (around 240 Roman soldiers plus their hangers-on).

While Tash was discovering her turf wall, I was reaching the deeper levels of my little test pit. The archaeology here was beautiful – pristine layers with no contamination from later periods. Under a deposit of soil containing medieval finds was a relatively sterile horizon that suggests the area was left

Tash finds a turf wall

The cross-hatching on this ceramic tells us it's from a box flue tile

fallow for some time, and beneath this, at long last, the Romans!

I first uncovered a layer of charcoal and burnt daub building material, with fragments of Roman pottery and animal bones. Lying beneath it was the stone foundation for a wall. Everything was consistent with the wall of a building within the fort, and based on its northern location, it had almost certainly been one of the barracks blocks, built on stone foundations, with the upper parts of the buildings made of wood and daub. All

that evidence for burning lying on top was telling the story of the last days of the fort. Had attackers started the fire, or did the Romans burn it down themselves before abandoning it to ensure that no valuable materials would fall into enemy hands?

The findings in my trench also helped to answer our question about the location of the Antonine Wall in Falkirk. If Trench 1 had been outside it, and my test pit was coming down onto an interior building, then the wall itself must have run between the two. This new alignment also fit far better with Marcus's ideas about following the lie of the land. When added to Tash's evidence that the fort had been smaller than originally thought, he was able to redraw the wall and the fort, forever changing our picture of this part of the Antonine Wall.

Leaving Falkirk, I reflected upon what an incredible piece of history we had just unearthed. Almost 2,000 years ago, the Roman army built a heavily fortified wall that divided local people from one another, simply because this was a conveniently narrow belt of land. I wondered whether the failure of this frontier had something to do with that lack of cultural insight on

My trench revealed the stone foundation of a barracks wall, and lots of evidence for the burning down of the buildings when they were abandoned

the part of the Romans. An entire generation would have grown up with this imposed division a part of their everyday lives, hearing tales of how it was before from their parents and grandparents.

To this day, I can remember as a child watching news reports about the fall of the Berlin Wall in 1989, 28 years after it was built, but a lifetime for those who were divided by it. The Antonine Wall fell twenty years after its construction began and a mere eight years after its completion – a startlingly relatable timeframe. It is incredible to me still that something so short-lived can echo through the centuries, jealously guarding its secrets beneath houses, bowling greens, and Girl Guide huts, until we come along with our trowels and spades to reveal them.

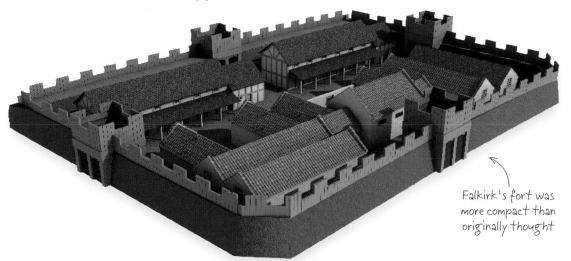

Falkirk's fort was more compact than originally thought

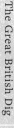

Glass Bottles

A surprising number of archaeologist friends of mine have told me that their interest in digging up the past first began with finding old glass bottles. Even if you only find a fragment of a glass bottle, you can probably work out quite a bit about it based upon its shape, colour, and any distinguishing features. Here are a few key things you can look for, to help you date your glass finds, and work out what contents they might originally have held.

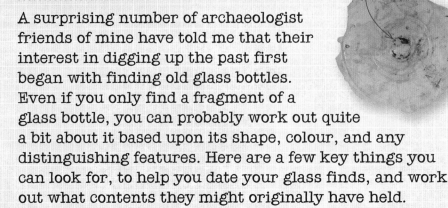

Glass bottle base, seen from below

Punty scar, a sign that you have hand-blown glass

These bottles, made on a mechanised production line, do not have punty scars

Hand-Blown Bottles

Until the late 19th century, glass bottles for drinks and other goods were blown individually by skilled glassblowers. Telltale marks of this 'hand-blown' glass include slightly uneven or bubbly glass and what is known as a 'punty' or 'pontil' scar on the base of the bottle, where the glass was transferred from a blowing iron to a rod that connected to the base while the glassblower worked the neck.

The form of the modern wine bottle developed slowly over time, from earlier, more rounded and squat vessels. Very dark green or brown bottles, sometimes known as 'black bottles', were made from the mid-17th century and were designed to protect their contents (often wine or beer) from sun damage.

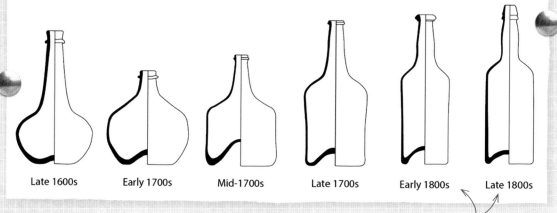

| Late 1600s | Early 1700s | Mid-1700s | Late 1700s | Early 1800s | Late 1800s |

If you find bottles or fragments with relatively straight sides, you are probably dealing with a bottle made in the 19th century or later

Signs of hand-blown glass

- Uneven form
- Bubbles in the glass
- Punty scar
- No vertical seam at the rim
- No embossed writing

Machine-Made Bottles

Mechanisation in glass bottle making took hold in the late 19th century. The simplest way to spot machine-made glass bottles is by looking for a vertical seam that runs all the way up the bottle, including the neck and rim. Seams can be present in glass that was hand-blown into moulds, but they do not usually continue right to the top of the vessel.

Machine-made glass bottles often bore embossed writing with the name of the drinks manufacturer and where they were based

Codd Bottles

These are among the most recognisable glass bottles. They were first introduced in 1872 by soft drink maker Hiram Codd of Camberwell and were designed specifically to hold carbonated (fizzy) drinks. They remained popular until the 1930s, at which point they declined in use.

The Codd bottle was designed to hold a marble and a rubber washer. The pressure of the gas in the fizzy drink forced the marble up against the washer, sealing it. To open the bottle, you would simply push the marble into a specially designed chamber.

Children would often smash the bottles after they were finished with in order to extract the marble!

A little piece of your author's family history

Small bottles

You may also uncover much smaller glass bottles used to contain medicine, essences, perfume and even poison from Victorian until recent times. They are often made of coloured glass, with interesting and beautiful forms.

111

WANT TO KNOW MORE?
Check out this website: **www.sha.org/bottle**

LAYING OUT YOUR TRENCH

So, you've done the background research, read up on safety and legal procedures, co-opted some household materials as tools, and hopefully even bought your own trowel! Now it's time to get down and dirty, and start your own archaeological dig.

Why do archaeologists go to the trouble of laying out neat trenches with right angled corners? It's not just that we're suckers for a bit of the old Pythagoras' theorem, that favourite of high school maths teachers (although there is a bit of that involved – see below).

The truth is that it is simply easier to see and – crucially – to record what we're doing if we maintain straight-sided, neat trenches. This way we can avoid the risk of more recent material from upper layers tumbling down into the early stuff and confusing us, and we can use the sides (baulks) of the trench in order to get a better look at the layers (stratigraphy) after we have excavated them. You will see first-hand how valuable this is when you come to record your trench.

Although there are heaps of fancy survey equipment out there, you can lay out a perfectly right-angled trench with just a few bits of string, some nails, and a cunning use of trigonometry; the maths of triangles. In this practical guide, I'll show you how to put theory into practice.

> **You will need**
> - Four long nails, or pegs
> - A tape measure (two if you have them)
> - String
> - Spade or turf-cutter
> - Tarpaulin

I highly recommend starting your archaeological career with a 1 x 1m trench, especially if you are working alone. This may seem small, but it is still a lot of work, and remember that the smaller the trench, the faster you will get past the topsoil and the more recent layers, and down to the good stuff. In a 1 x 1m trench, the diagonal line should measure 1m 41cm (1.41m).

> **HOT TIP!** If you only have one tape, you can take a piece of string and pre-mark it to the correct length.

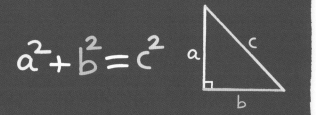

Pythagoras' theorem:
"In a right-angled triangle, the square on the hypotenuse is equal to the sum of the squares on the other two sides."

What this means in practice is that we can make a right-angle just by measuring out certain key lengths.

$$a^2 + b^2 = c^2$$

1 Decide where you'd like your trench to be, and drive a long nail or peg into one of the corners – it should be secure, but not so deep that you can't fix the end of your tape to it. Now take the tape and hold it firmly at this point, with the nail on '0'. Draw the tape out to the 1m mark.

The baseline for your trench

Find the 1m mark

2 Check that the orientation of the tape is consistent with where you'd like the side of the trench to be, and then – keeping it taut – drive another nail in at the 1m mark. Now you have the baseline for your trench.

HOT TIP! It's best to co-opt some help from a neighbour or family member for this part, but if you have to do this alone, you can use bulldog clips to secure the tape in place.

3 Now it's time to locate the other two corners of your trench. Ask somebody to hold one tape to each of the two nails you have already driven into the ground, making sure they stay on the '0' mark. Draw the two tapes out in the direction you'd like to place your trench.

Hold one tape at '0' on each of the two nails

The corner is located at the intersection between 1m and 1.41m

4 Measure out to 1m on tape 1, and 1.41m on tape 2, and hold them at these points. Now, keeping the tapes low to the ground so they are level, move them until the '1m' mark on tape 1 meets the '1.41 m' mark on tape 2. Drive a nail into this exact location.

Now we just do the same, but the other way around. Keeping the tapes held to the same two baseline nails, find the 1m mark on the longer tape (previously our 1.41m tape), and extend the shorter one out from 1m to 1.41m. Finding the intersection between these will give you the final corner of your trench.

5 It's important to double check that the length of each side is 1m to within a reasonable margin of error (you can get away with an error of 1–2cm). If they are not, then you must go back to the previous stage and try again. Once you're happy that you have a nice, square trench, take some string and wrap it tightly round the nails at the four corners. This will give you a clear, straight line to work from as you start to dig.

your trench, you may lose the grass beneath it.

The soil in your garden has a lot of weight above it and will be very compacted. As you remove it, it will be loosened and will increase in volume, so you're likely to find that your spoil heap is a lot bigger than you expect!

Now that you have a nice, neat square or rectangle pegged out, and a ready spot to pile your spoil, you can begin to remove the top layer of soil. If you are digging in your lawn, I highly recommend using a sharp spade, or a turf-cutter tool, to cut a line around the edge of the trench. Follow the line of the string, and ensure it stays taut. Once you have done this, you can start to cut the interior of the trench into smaller squares, and then lever these out using the spade or shovel. Pile the turf squares up somewhere separate to your main spoil heap, so that you can replace them after you backfill the trench. After de-turfing, or (if you are digging in flowerbeds) removing the top few inches of soil, use your archaeologist's trowel to clean up the sides of the trench.

WANT TO GO BIGGER?

If you have a large garden and a lot of helpers, you may want to lay out a 2 x 1m trench. In that case, your diagonal should measure 2m 24cm. Lay out a baseline of 2m in length, and then follow the procedure described above, with the tapes meeting at 1m and 2.24m respectively.

SPOILER ALERT!

Before you start digging, make sure that you have considered where you will be putting the soil you take out (otherwise known as the spoil heap). If you have a tarpaulin available, this is ideal and will protect your garden from damage. If you are planning to keep the trench open for just a few days, it is best to put the tarpaulin on the lawn beside the spoil heap, but be aware that if left for more than 3–4 days before backfilling

THE CONQUEROR'S CASTLE

WEST DERBY, LIVERPOOL

What comes to mind when you imagine a castle? I suspect that for most of us the answer is a large stone structure, perhaps with multiple turrets, a water-filled moat, and a drawbridge. The earliest castles, however, would have looked rather different. So-called 'motte and bailey' structures consisted of an enclosed settlement (the bailey) and a large mound of earth (the motte) topped by a wooden or stone building (the keep), where the Lord and his family resided.

For around 200 years this was the dominant type of castle in Britain, but few survive. Some fell out of use and were abandoned, while others were rebuilt using stone and more elaborate architecture, hiding the traces of the early structure beneath. A fine example of this is Windsor Castle, which has remained a royal residence almost continually since the 11th century and has seen almost as many building extensions and architectural changes

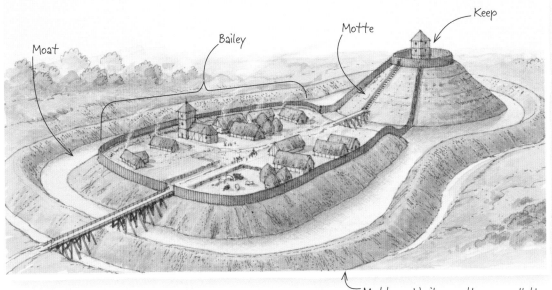

Moat

Bailey

Motte

Keep

Motte and bailey castles were all the rage for 11th century conquerors as it has monarchs.

One of the best-known people in English history was a Frenchman who lived over 900 years ago. I'm referring to William Duke of Normandy, otherwise known as William the Conqueror, or William the Bastard (in reference to his parentage rather than his personality!). When William battled and defeated Harold Godwinson to become King

of England in 1066, he needed to secure his hold over the territory he had taken, and thus began a programme of rapid motte and bailey castle-building. The advantage of motte and bailey castles is that they can be constructed relatively quickly – in just a few weeks if you have access to enough labour – and making a mound of earth requires considerably less skill and calculation than engineering monumental stone architecture. These castles were built to be defensive strongholds, but their height also made them

a bold statement of power in the landscape.

In what is becoming a bit of a recurring theme in the *Great British Dig*, we met up with Hugh in a pub garden. This time, Tash, Richard and I were keen to explain why we had brought him to West Derby, which – in spite of its slightly misleading name – is a suburb of Liverpool. Although you wouldn't know it today, this peaceful residential area had once been the site of its very own Norman motte and bailey castle, the last above-ground remains of which were levelled

I'm getting peaty undertones with a moaty top note – Hugh discovers that waterlogged soils can have distinctive smells

in the late 20th century. It was built in 1100 by a certain Roger de Poitou (or at least, it was built by various less fortunate people on behalf of the illustrious Roger). The castle would have acted as a stronghold, helping the Normans to subdue rebellious locals, and – perhaps with this in mind – they chose to construct it in a location that already had a gravitational sense of power: the site of a royal hunting lodge.

While the keep at West Derby was long since lost to the ravages of time, the castle's motte had managed to survive as a noticeable earthwork for almost 900 years until it was finally razed. All our hopes thus rested on being able to trace the outer defensive ditch surrounding the bailey, more commonly known as the moat. Although the moat had long since been filled in, we hoped to detect characteristic soil changes that would help us to trace where it had once been.

While we set about opening our trenches, environmental archaeologist Don O'Meara

was busy readying his hand core. Given that we can't exactly go about digging up entire neighbourhoods, one of our key strategies at this site was the use of geological coring (see Dig 10 for a full description of how this technique works – page 174). Like a soil sommelier with an insane, oversized corkscrew, Don repeatedly wound his instrument into the ground and pulled it out again with a tube of soil trapped within, allowing him to build up a picture of the different layers under his feet. By doing this at selected locations across the site, we hoped to combine his findings with the evidence from the trenches to work out just how wide and deep that elusive moat had been, as well as using its location to help pin down the size of the original castle it enclosed.

Luckily for those of us who were keen on digging something a bit more extensive than Don's cores, the local residents had been so amenable that we were able to open three

trenches in neighbouring gardens, as well as one large one in the communal green that had once housed the surviving remains of the motte.

Until we put spade to ground, of course, we can never be sure what period of time we will meet, as was shown eloquently in one of the aforementioned three gardens, at the home of Amie, Dave, and their two daughters. Here, our discoveries told a most unexpected and fascinating story about West Derby in the 20th century. We uncovered the remains of a tent peg, a toy soldier and an imitation gemstone from some costume jewellery. Somehow this collection of finds transported me to a pleasant vision

A somewhat dirty Don wields his trusty hand core

Sitting in the remains of an air raid shelter, imagining what it must have been like to live in heavily-bombed Liverpool during the Second World War

unexpected turn of events – the remains of an air raid shelter under this unassuming lawn. I was reminded now of the many disrupted childhoods that had been truncated by the grim reality of warfare. The toy soldier suddenly seemed less innocent, as I chatted with the children who lived here today about how the residents of Liverpool – an important port city – had been hit heavily by air raids during the Second World War.

We were joined in Dig HQ by medieval expert Dr Rachel Swallow, who wasted

of growing up camping out and playing in the garden, perhaps at the start of one of those wonderful, long summer holidays of childhood, when it seems that the free time ahead is almost infinite in its potential.

A jarring note was introduced to these musings, however, by the discovery of a bullet dating to 1941, and – in a completely

no time in whisking Hugh off to nearby Cheshire to visit the site of Halton Castle. This motte and bailey castle had managed to survive rather better above ground than the one we were investigating at West Derby and was now – rather wonderfully – the site of a pub garden. Standing in what was once the bailey of Halton Castle gave a genuine sense

A connection with the past: the boys went home and ransacked their own toy collections to find the 21st century versions of the soldiers we dug up

Halton Castle, now a beer garden

Dr Rachel Swallow takes Hugh on a visit to Halton Castle

of how enormous it would originally have been, and how different this little point in the landscape would have felt at the time, filled as it must have been with stables, kitchens, houses, barracks, bakeries and warehouses.

Rachel explained to Hugh that the motte would have been a lot steeper and a lot higher when first constructed in the 11th century; the largest examples were over 24 metres high. This height provided a fantastic vantage point over the surrounding area for the Lord, allowing him to spot trouble from miles away, control trade and showcase his power over the surrounding landscape.

Rachel's insights threw up a whole range of questions that only added to the mystery of the moat at West Derby. Would it have been water-filled, calmly reflecting the sunlight, or was it one of Rachel's dry moats, with sharp wooden stakes in its base to wound hapless attackers? How wide and deep was it, and how far did it extend? Although of interest in themselves, any answers to these

questions would also tell us more about the size and layout of the castle itself.

With the question of height still hot in his mind, Hugh sought out the tallest accomplice he could find – our very own Richard – and persuaded him to head up to the top of the nearby church, St Mary's. Here, they were able to gain some sense of the impressive vantage point from West Derby's castle, as well as a brilliant perspective over the areas being excavated by our team.

Somewhat reluctantly, I think, Richard eventually acknowledged that he and Hugh had seen all they could see from the church, and he headed back to continue his geophysical survey on the green. We had hoped to use geophysics to identify the previous location of the moat, but Richard was becoming increasingly frustrated with

Building tall provided a good vantage point for defence, and made a statement of power over the local populace

his lack of success. Although it appears that there had been too much modern disturbance in this area to capture sight of the moat using geophysics, he did notice something rather telling: a little dip in the garden wall of local residents Brian and Barbara.

Why would anybody be interested in a dip in someone else's garden wall, you might ask? The answer is that this dip was an important clue to the location of the original moat. While the moat itself had long since been filled in, the soil that had filled it had simply not had the time to become as compact as the material it was dug out of, and would be richer in organic materials that rot away and leave soil darker and softer. When a person

'Hey Richard, that's not how you hold a mag!' – Rich heads off for a sandwich

Tash's fragment of medieval pottery was the first clue that we were going to find the moat

builds, say, a garden wall, the weight of the wall will press down further into this more recent soil, and over time this will create a dip in the ground surface.

As brilliant as Richard's insight into the wall location was, we were still concerned that we simply weren't finding enough evidence for the moat. Tash had stayed fairly quiet as she worked with expert archaeologist Robin in the large trench on the green, but as we sat down mid-week to mull over our findings, it turned out she had uncovered some medieval pottery – a hopeful sign that we might be hitting the layers we needed. She was also pretty sure that they had started to hit the top of the filled-in moat.

Meanwhile, I had been encountering some watery features of my own, working alongside expert archaeologists Nathan and Alice in the two gardens close to where we found an air raid shelter. The middle of these gardens, belonging to retired couple Jim and Marie, was particularly waterlogged, which was puzzling – did the moat extend out further than previously thought, or was this evidence for some other feature?

As usual, the answer to my questions was that we needed to get out there and do a bit more digging, but it wasn't one any of us particularly relished, because digging in

Crossbows allowed people to fire powerful shots over incredible distances...

waterlogged features is really difficult. No sooner have you bailed out the water than it starts to seep back in, and you lose sight of the feature you were working on. I hoped that the archaeology we needed to find wouldn't be too much further down.

While Hugh went off to learn more about medieval warfare with weapons expert Tod Cutler, Tash, Richard and I returned to our investigation, desperate to solve the mystery of this elusive moat. Just as the situation in Jim and Marie's garden was becoming too watery to manage, we hit upon a massive structure that began to make some sense of what we had

found. When I had first knocked on Jim's door, he had mentioned the difficulties he and Marie experienced with gardening, due to persistent waterlogging. Although we couldn't wave a magic wand and resolve this problem for Jim and Marie, we were at last able to explain to the long-suffering

Water, water, everywhere, and not a drop to drink

...although I'm hoping Hugh wasn't actually aiming at me!

couple just *why* they had so many problems with their roses. For what we had uncovered was a very large, very well-built culvert (underground drainage system), of the sort used in 17th and 18th century agriculture.

After a chat with Rachel, I discovered that there was historical evidence for a mill, with associated millponds, in this very area, which was medieval in origin but remained in use until at least the later 16th century. To date this feature, we used what I refer to as a 'time sandwich'. The culvert was put in to drain the millponds, so can't have been from earlier than the 16th century, when the mill was still in use. Sealing it above was a

layer full of 19th century finds. Piecing this evidence together, I was fairly confident that it was built in the 17th or 18th century. Our concerns that the moat was located in the wrong place had been completely brushed aside; what we had found, instead, was evidence for the continuing use and

Expert Robin records the archaeology of the moat

Taking rough measurements of the depth of the archaeological layers from the surface to compare with Don's coring results

reshaping of this landscape in the centuries after the castle was abandoned.

Tash's enormous trench on the green was finally proving its worth, and – along with the results of Don's coring escapades – was allowing us to literally redraw the map of West Derby's 900-year-old motte and bailey castle. They had indeed found the moat, and – having been able to excavate out some of the material that had filled it after it fell out of use – could confirm that it had rather an unusual shape! It was around 9 metres wide, most probably because it had also had to be rather shallow.

Why shallow? Because of the same problems we had faced in Jim and Marie's garden: this area has a very high water table, meaning that the ground is saturated in water from as little as about 1 metre down. The Normans had recognised this and adapted their designs accordingly, creating a formidable wet moat that made up for in width what

it lacked in depth. Later, the farmers who reclaimed this land in the 17th and 18th centuries had been forced to construct monumental drainage systems to drain the millponds and deal with the high water table. And now, in the 21st century, Jim struggled to keep his roses from root-rot.

We had come to Liverpool seeking a moat, and a moat we had found. Yet more impressively, our brief investigation had allowed us to redraw the map of the ancient motte and bailey castle that once stood here, showing that it had been more extensive than was previously assumed. Like all great adventures, however, the journey we underwent at West Derby taught us things we had never thought to ask. We came away with a richly illustrated picture of the ebb and flow of life in this small corner of the world during a span of more than 900 years. It had gone from forested hunting lodge, to rude statement of power over a newly conquered landscape, to peaceful and prosperous agricultural land, and then once more to

defensive location in 1939, when struck by a war, the destructive scale of which none of its medieval inhabitants could surely have imagined.

Today, this place is the focus of a warm and welcoming community, with residents of all ages enjoying the green that was once the site of a formidable castle, but who knows what the future may hold? If West Derby had taught us anything, it was that the course of history twists and turns, and that while even the most serene of landscapes may one day become theatres of war, the reverse is also true: sites of bloody conquest and devastation can transform yet rapidly into the playgrounds of a new generation of children, marked only to future archaeologists by the fleeting loss of a tent peg or a small toy soldier.

We redrew the map of West Derby's motte and bailey castle, and showed how the site had changed over time

Medieval Pottery

Early Medieval Pottery
In the early medieval period, pots tended to be fairly roughly made, looking similar to some of the later prehistoric types. The sherds can be thick and sometimes have a cork-like texture in the cross-section.

Crushed shells, used to strengthen this pottery against changes in heat during firing and cooking

Shelly ware, 9th–10th century AD

Later Medieval Pottery
From around the time of William the Conqueror (late 11th Century), pottery became more elaborate. The most common types of medieval pottery remains found by archaeologists are storage vessels, cooking pots and jugs. Don't expect to find much evidence for the plates and bowls that people would have eaten from, though, as these were mostly made of wood.

One of the most distinctive types of medieval pottery found throughout Britain is Green Glazed Ware, which was often used to make jugs and other serving vessels.

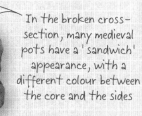

Fragment of a medieval pottery handle

In the broken cross-section, many medieval pots have a 'sandwich' appearance, with a different colour between the core and the sides

Green glazed pottery

Often, much of the glaze has corroded away so you will only find traces of it

Common Types

Medieval pottery varies a lot from region to region, so what you might find depends heavily on where you live. To help you get started, here are some of the broad types that are common across large parts of Britain.

Stamford ware was manufactured in Lincolnshire up to the 13th century – when we find this type of pottery, it is usually robust and functional with simple decoration

Brandsby ware is a relatively common but still beautiful find in the north of England and particularly in Yorkshire

Note the characteristic mottled green glaze

You can recognise Cistercian ware by its deep-brown, metallic-looking glaze

Cistercian ware jug handle, late medieval to early post-medieval

Note the pale clay, with flecks of grit inclusions

Coarse Border ware is particularly common in south east England, but it is typical of many of the medieval and Tudor pottery types found across the UK

Into the Tudor period, the green glaze used on pottery became deeper in colour and more vibrant

ALL ABOUT SOIL

How often do you stop to think about the earth beneath your feet? And when you do think about it, do you imagine it as something fixed and static, or as a constantly churning, moving medium, teeming with life?

We speak of wanting to plant our feet on 'solid ground', but there really is no such thing. Our entire planet has developed to constantly recycle itself, with the molten part of its core rising up to create new rocks, which erode into soils and are churned by worms and human ploughs, quietly feeding vital water and nutrients to the roots of plants as their leaves stretch up to the sun, and greedily drawing them back down again, after the plants and the animals that ate them die and decompose.

Having some knowledge of soil is crucial before starting any excavation, because we need to understand how the layers we dig through built up over time, and to recognise what is natural, and what stems from human activity. Happily for the would-be archaeologist, there are a few handy tips to get you started in understanding what lies beneath, which will help you to identify what you are seeing as you dig down through the layers.

SOIL HORIZONS

Any soil that has been around for a while will show characteristic changes in colour, texture,

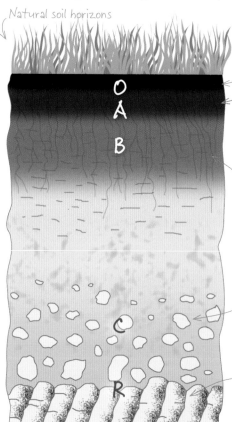

Natural soil horizons

O
A
B
C
R

Organic (O) – mainly dead plants, in various stages of decomposition.

Topsoil (A) – minerals and organic material, typically with lots of root and worm activity. Identify it by its (usually) dark colour and organic smell.

Subsoil (B) – contains minerals (e.g. iron) filtered down from A Horizon. Less rich in organic material. Identify it by its lighter colour, or the tinge of the minerals (e.g. orange/red for iron oxide).

Substratum (C) – largely made up of weathered bedrock. Identify it by the presence of lots of sharp rock fragments.

Bedrock (R) – what type of rock this is and how deep it lies depends on your local geology. Identify it by not being able to dig through it!

and even smell as you dig through it.

All this seems relatively straightforward, but remember we are dealing with archaeology here, and human beings tend to complicate things. When digging archaeology, you can expect to find many more layers, and they won't always be neatly horizontal. You may encounter imported soils (check out the geology of your local area – see Researching Your Local Area, page 46),

How to spot a Bronze Age pit

Understanding how to recognise and describe different soils will help you to identify archaeological features as well as natural ones. This is crucial for many periods, but especially for British prehistory, as most remains of structures such as buildings are only indicated today by soil changes.

In this example from our dig in Stretton, the darker soil within the circle told us that somebody had cut a pit into the sandy ground, which was later filled in with a different soil.

We suspected that the line of pits at Stretton was Bronze Age based on comparisons with other archaeological sites, and this was confirmed by a Bronze Age find at the base of one of them!

While the difference between the two soils is only just about visible in this image, it is very noticeable when digging, because the texture of the soil filling the pit is very different to the stuff around it.

This was the original Bronze Age ground surface, into which the pit was cut. It is sandier, more compacted, lighter and more reddish in colour, and has fewer stones in it.

The material that filled in the pit felt very different to dig. It was more clayey, and not as well sorted, with more stones in it.

demolition layers, burnt material, foundation cuts and in situ building foundations.

Sometimes, we even find buried A-B soil horizons, when human or natural processes have resulted in a large amount of material being deposited over the original surface, sealing it in. Don't worry if this seems too much to take in: the key is to record what you find, so you can continue to analyse and interpret it later.

DESCRIBING SOIL

There is no better training for the would-be archaeologist than sitting down and examining some soil. With a few simple tests, you can pin down what type of soil is in a particular layer, and whether it is different from the layers above and below.

Start off by taking a sample of your soil – something about the width of a 50p coin should be enough. If the soil is very dry, moisten it. This is to ensure that you are always comparing the soils themselves, and not the changing weather when you dug them up.

Check out the example of soil description in the table below, then use the following charts and guides to try it for yourself.

Layer Number	Composition	Compaction	Colour	Inclusions
103	Silty clay	Plastic	Mid-brown	10% large angular grit, 5% charcoal, some flecks of shell

Checklist
- ☐ Composition
- ☐ Compaction
- ☐ Colour
- ☐ Inclusions

COMPOSITION (WHAT THE SOIL IS MADE UP OF)

There are three main soil textures: clay, sand, and silt. Most soils in Britain are a combination of these types, and learning to distinguish them is a key part of archaeological training.

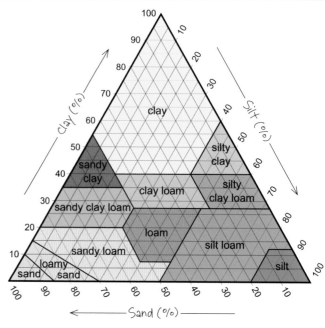

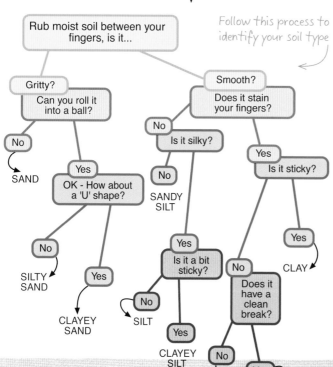

Follow this process to identify your soil type

COMPACTION (HOW LOOSE OR TOUGH THE SOIL IS)

LOOSE – your sample falls apart upon handling

FRIABLE – your sample breaks with a small amount of pressure

FIRM – it takes a lot of pressure to break your sample

HARD – you can't crush your sample using your fingers

PLASTIC – you can squeeze and shape your sample without it breaking

INCLUSIONS

Use this chart to estimate the percentage of a soil that is taken up by inclusions (e.g. flecks of charcoal)

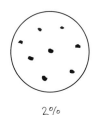 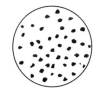

2%   10%   25%   70%

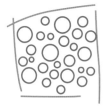   

Use this chart to estimate how well sorted your deposit is (i.e. is there much difference in particle size?)

Very well-sorted   Well-sorted   Moderately well-sorted   Poorly sorted

Use this ruler to describe the size of pebbles

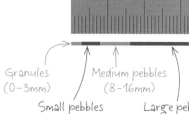

Granules (0–3mm)

Small pebbles (3–8mm)

Medium pebbles (8–16mm)

Large pebbles (16–32mm)

Very large pebbles (32–64mm)

Recording the type and extent of the layers

GARDENS OF POWER

BENINGBROUGH, YORKSHIRE

'Well, this is one of the poshest back gardens I've ever seen,' quipped Hugh upon arriving at the National Trust property of Beningbrough Hall on a gloriously hot summer's day in North Yorkshire. While other visitors to the site ate ice creams and leisurely explored the splendid gardens, we had something very different in mind: a good, old-fashioned bit of hard physical labour.

The hall itself was built by the Bourchier family more than 300 years ago. Completed in 1716, its architecture dates right to the start of the Georgian era. Impressive as it is, this building was never intended to be seen in isolation from the extensive gardens surrounding it: in the traditions of the day, house, gardens and outbuildings would all have contributed to one grand statement about the Bourchiers.

Yet what visitors to the site see today is the result of a vast programme of 19th

century remodelling. The Hall itself is an isolated remnant of the original design, stranded in a beautiful, yet altogether alien landscape to the one in which it was conceived. For once, we were not only digging in gardens, but looking for them, too.

Gardening. Integral to the *Great British Dig*, of course, but also a significant part of British culture and identity. Even those of us who don't have our own gardens grow up surrounded by ideas about them. Who hasn't at some point walked past somebody else's beautifully-maintained patch of green and experienced a smidgeon of envy? While many of us garden for pleasure, we also do it for display, and the same was eminently true of the extensive gardens belonging to the great houses of the 17th to 19th centuries. Prestigious families were under pressure to maintain their social standing, display

their taste and pedigree, and entertain their guests in style. As well as being multi-layered visual statements of taste and wealth, the gardens surrounding great houses were social spaces that would have played a large role in many formal (and perhaps a few less formal!) activities.

We had been invited to dig here by indefatigable National Trust archaeologist Mark Newman. Bouncing on his heels in boyish anticipation, Mark could hardly

The National Trust's
Mark Newman

wait to lend a hand in solving the mysteries of Beningbrough's lost gardens. He also entertained us with the history of garden fashions, explaining that throughout the 18th and early 19th centuries, and thanks to individuals such as Lancelot 'Capability' Brown, the older tradition of small, formal gardens gave way to larger-scale, 'naturalistic' (but in fact carefully curated) landscapes.

I remember thinking that if they had built their gardens to go with the house, the Bourchier family must have been kicking themselves; surely this was the equivalent of spending a fortune replacing your entire music collection with MiniDiscs in the late '90s, and then getting home and seeing an advert for these new-fangled MP3 players. In any case, perhaps it really did

sting, because the remodelling of the grounds at Beningbrough to the more naturalistic style did not take place until sometime in the later 19th century, after the estate had been inherited by a new family – the Dawnays – who unfortunately left almost no records of the process.

And, in a nutshell, that was our remit – 'Hello Hugh, Chloe, Richard and Tash.

Ken has been a volunteer at Beningbrough for 15 years, and was keen to learn more about the lost gardens

Could you grab a digger and some archaeologists, and reconstruct the entire lost grounds of an 18th century stately home?' And of course, we said yes.

One of the things I adore about archaeology is that it's a true game of strategy. To solve the mystery of Beningbrough's lost gardens, we would need a careful combination of wide and close perspectives. A key piece of evidence to our advantage was a recent map of the house and grounds that had been created by a technique known as 'LiDAR' (see page 237), which shows up large-scale features such as ancient plough marks, buried water-courses and building foundations – intriguing clues to what lies beneath.

We identified areas for geophysical survey using magnetometry and resistivity, both of which rely on passing signals through the ground and reading how they are distorted when they bounce back. Trenches would help to date the features we were seeing and to 'ground truth' (test) our interpretations of the survey data. We also called upon geoarchaeologist Kris Krawiec, who had

Richard uses magnetometry to pick up traces of buried garden features such as paths and partitions

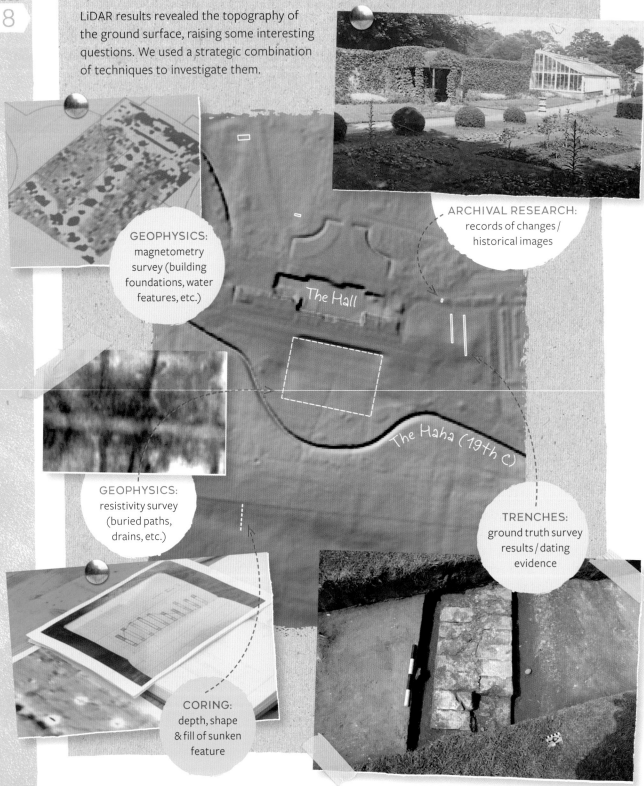

LiDAR results revealed the topography of the ground surface, raising some interesting questions. We used a strategic combination of techniques to investigate them.

GEOPHYSICS: magnetometry survey (building foundations, water features, etc.)

ARCHIVAL RESEARCH: records of changes / historical images

The Hall

The Haha (19th C)

GEOPHYSICS: resistivity survey (buried paths, drains, etc.)

TRENCHES: ground truth survey results / dating evidence

CORING: depth, shape & fill of sunken feature

worked with us in Lenton, to take a series of soil cores cutting across a mysterious sunken feature to the south of the house (see page 174).

With various survey techniques well underway, and Richard handling the geophysics, Tash paired up with Mandy, one of our talented team of archaeologists. With the help of a mechanical digger, they opened a large trench to the north-west of the hall, where the LiDAR had picked out a series of features that we hoped might link to a lost stable block.

Our expectations of finding structural building remains in this trench were increased early on, when Tash found a beautiful handmade brick of just the sort we would associate with the 18th century phase of

the hall. Unfortunately, things went rapidly downhill from there, as a lower layer turned up a rather different brick, confirmed by finds expert Dr David Griffiths as dating to the early 19th century. Undeterred, Tash rolled up her sleeves and ploughed ahead. It was back to the drawing board for Trench 1.

Poor David. Although his true passion

Geoarchaeologist Kris Krawiec uses scientific techniques to understand how sites are built up over time

Expert archaeologist Mandy contemplates her next move as the digger opens Trench 1

and 6 pennies per thousand bricks. Not to be outdone, brickmakers immediately began to increase the size of their bricks, eventually causing the government to respond in 1801 by setting the maximum dimensions of a brick to 10 x 5 x 3 inches. Rather wonderfully, our brick was just shy of these limits, demonstrating that people in Britain have always been at their most ingenious when faced with the twin prospects of saving a few bob, and getting one over on the government!

is for the Romans, he seems to spend most of his time handling badly-behaved bricks. Perhaps he only has himself to blame, given that he weaves such wonderful histories around them, and this brick was no exception.

Among the more creative property tax initiatives of British government over the centuries was the so-called 'brick tax'. Introduced in 1784, it set a levy of 2 shillings

While Tash and David were agonising over bricks, I had joined fellow archaeologists Nathan, Alice and Ayesha in a charming

Not just another brick in the wall

Some people think the cauliflower more beautiful than the rose, but I've always loved the unassuming charm of wildflowers

walled garden to the east of the Hall, today resplendent with borders of wild flowers. Historical sources, including a handful of black and white photos, told us that from the late 19th century this had been a rose garden, but they left no clue to what was here before then. We wanted to know if the earlier gardens had extended to this area, and if so, what had they looked like?

Richard had somehow managed to wrangle himself a chat with National Trust Curator Matthew Constantine, who became

We drummed up some help from residents of the local villages, National Trust volunteers, and a young family who live in the old gardener's cottage on the estate

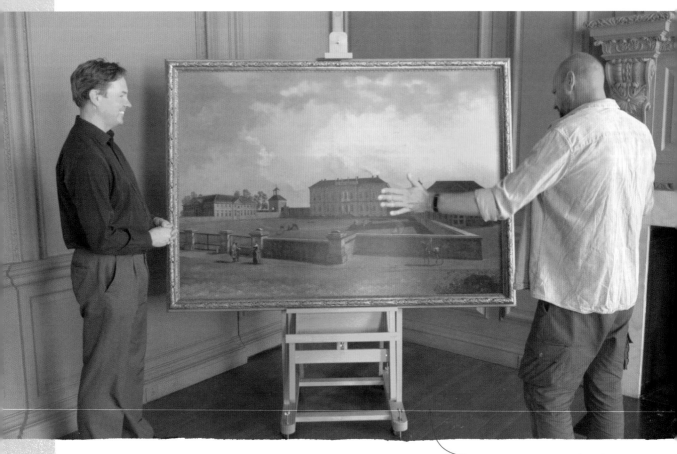

How much could we trust the depiction of the hall in this 1751 painting?

his personal guide to one of the most important clues in our slender volume of historical sources on Beningbrough Hall: a painting made of the hall in 1751, only 35 years after it was completed. The painting would have been hung in the Bourchier family townhouse, just to be sure that any visitors knew how impressive their country estate was. It depicted two rather large service blocks – most likely stables – on either side of the main approach to the hall, but neither of these survives today. We had placed Trench 1 in the hope of finding them, but as Tash had already discovered, this trench had its own ideas.

While Richard mulled over the lost stable blocks, I pursued a burgeoning obsession of my own: the 200-metre-long, straight,

apparently sunken feature to the south of the house. Its regularity suggested some form of decorative canal, but that didn't quite fit with the layout, because it ran parallel with the house, and was located at the rear rather than the front.

Mark showed me a sketch of the house drawn by topographical engineer Samuel Buck in 1720. Buck was more interested in the lands surrounding the house than the building itself, and to save time he only sketched one side of the house and gardens, trusting to the rigid symmetry of the age. When we held up a mirror to the drawing, the original 18th century vista popped out before our eyes, complete with extensive formal gardens running to a long, linear feature dubbed a 'fine channel'. For many years, Mark explained, it had been assumed that Buck's drawing was somewhat fanciful and the channel was his invention, but the recently LiDAR data seemed to support the authenticity of his depiction.

Kris's coring confirmed that our linear feature was the remains of a canal, rather shallow and wide, and just the sort of thing that would have been used as a decorative feature in a 17th century formal garden. The reason it was aligned so unusually was that it had been constructed to run out from the original Bourchier residence, a far more modest dwelling built in 1556.

Much to Mark's excitement, our evidence was beginning to align with a pet theory of his: that the orientation of the Hall was designed to match existing gardens, belonging to the Elizabethan manor. If Mark was correct – and it increasingly seemed to

be the case – then the Hall was built to match the gardens, and not the other way around!

Tash had already discovered that her trench was not quite as – ahem – *stable* as she and Richard had first hoped. Indeed, as excavation continued it became apparent that some features on the LiDAR map, which we had originally taken to be associated with the stables, had been caused by a line of large ornamental ponds, one of which was right under Tash's trench. It seems that we were looking at the north-west corner of the formal gardens, which made them far more extensive than originally thought.

As unexpected and exciting as this was, the mystery of the stables remained

By mirroring Buck's original sketch (the right half of this image) we were able to gain a sense of the symmetry and grandeur of the early hall and its gardens

Mark shows me Buck's 1720 sketch

unsolved. It was time to revisit the painting. Digital finds expert Marcus did some calculations and suggested an alternative projection for the lost buildings, so Richard took a gamble on a last minute test pit, and – bingo! – hit evidence for what had once been the foundation of a substantial wall.

The bricks themselves had been removed, and the whole thing was filled in and then sealed by a thick layer of clay that looks to have been imported to the site. It seems that the 19th century reconfiguration of the gardens had seen the careful demolition of the stables, the reuse of their building materials, and the importation of vast quantities of landscaping materials to seal their remains.

Over in the former rose garden, we were also making ground – or should I say, taking ground? I had been working at the top end of one of our long, thin trenches along with Nathan and his parents, who were visiting for the day, when we started to uncover a line of handmade bricks set into what looked like

the top of a very well-preserved wall.

We don't often find the *tops* of walls in archaeology. Most commonly, we find their foundations, which would have been cut into the earth, and which may (or may not, as Richard found above) contain surviving bricks and mortar. I decided to go deeper within a smaller section of the trench to investigate the depth of the wall, which revealed itself to be beautifully built, with solid, expert bonding. It had not bowed or

Hugh, Tash and Mark consider how the ponds relate to the hall

David confirming the early date of the bricks in my trench

buckled, or lost a brick in all these centuries. At about 1 metre down, the little pit I had sunk began to fill with water, and I was obliged to stick my arm in and feel my way to check we had reached the base.

I was forming an idea about what the wall had been for, but in order to confirm my suspicions I had to investigate its relationship to the surrounding soil on the other side. Having done so, I was confident that this had been a terracing wall, built to allow the garden to be split between two levels, the lower of which was a sunken garden. This interpretation was reinforced when we caught traces of the same wall in the second of our long trenches.

Perhaps it was too daunting a prospect to destroy such well-built walls, or perhaps they provided a useful framework, but for whatever reason, the architects of the gardens' 19th century remodelling chose to add just enough soil to create a gentle, naturalistic slope here, where once there

The buried 17th century wall

Surely one of the finds of the season was this incredibly well-preserved moulded plasterwork

had been a formal division between walkway and gardens.

While digging along the top of what would have been the walkway of the sunken garden, we happened upon the icing on the cake: two rather large and well-preserved fragments

of moulded plaster. Knowing Mark to be somewhere in the vicinity, I have to confess that rather than reaching for a radio I just hollered out for him. Together we excitedly turned the plaster over in our hands. Traces of paint survived on one piece – it looked to me like a pale blue sky. These were entirely in keeping with the interior decoration of a fanciful 17th or 18th century garden building, such as a teahouse. 'Just the sort of thing you might find at the end of a walkway along a

We were able to reconstruct the layout of the original formal gardens, built before the hall itself

sunken garden,' bubbled Mark, happily.

Our time at Beningbrough demonstrated the immense power of combining different investigative techniques, from historical drawings, paintings and photographs, to aerial survey, geophysics, coring and excavation. We were able to reveal the true extent of the original 17th century gardens, and to provide insights into their design and layout. We had demonstrated that the hall itself was probably built to remain in line with the gardens, and had found direct evidence for original buildings and garden features.

The conventions of the English language can be misleading. When I write of the Bourchier and Dawnay families making changes to the Beningbrough Hall estate it almost gives the impression they were personally rolling up their sleeves and shifting earth! Visit the property today, however, and you will see just how many gardeners it takes to maintain its beauty. It's a year-round, all-weather job: planting spring-blooming bulbs before the frost sets in, protecting plants from pests, pruning, trimming, germinating, feeding, watering, and digging, digging, digging.

Yet I doubt that even today's population of diligent gardeners could meet the demand of labour it must have taken to maintain the grandeur of those complex, partitioned 17th century gardens, which we found to have been even more extensive than previously thought. Later, the whole estate must have become an enormous, highly organised construction site, as it was reworked to meet the new fashion for naturalistic landscapes. A huge quantity of clay was brought in to seal earlier features, while all traces of the old formality such as the walkway and sunken garden were carefully hidden under gentle, sloping forms that belied the extent to which they had been deliberately constructed and maintained by many generations of careful and hard-working hands, right up to the present day. Let us hope there will be many more.

Metals

Rusted iron nails, 20th century

In 1816, Danish museum director Christian Jürgensen Thomsen went against the grain by organising his prehistoric collections according to what objects were found together rather than, for example, putting all of the spearheads into one case.

To help with this classification, Thomsen divided prehistory into three broad epochs, based on what he saw as the prevailing technologies of the time: the Stone Age, the Bronze Age and the Iron Age.

Thomsen's focus on weapons and cutting tools reflects when he lived: a time of industrial revolution, where the importance of steel to machinery and transport infrastructure was paramount. It also reflects what survives in the ground more than what mattered to people living in prehistory. I still remember my university lecturer Hamish Forbes informing us that the vast majority of human history had in fact been the 'Wood Age'.

Prehistoric Metal By 'Prehistoric Metal' I don't mean the sort of music that our James Wright probably listens to of a nostalgic Sunday morning, but any archaeological find of metal that belongs to the Roman period or earlier. You are highly unlikely to discover any ancient metalwork while digging in your back garden, but just in case you do, it is important to know that UK law obliges you to report anything it defines as 'treasure' to the Coroner's Office within 14 days of discovery. Reporting your find ensures that you have legal rights over it (shared with the landowner, if you have permission to dig on somebody else's land), and that it can be properly recorded by the Portable Antiquities Scheme (see page 232).

Medieval and Later Metal

From the medieval period onwards, the everyday metal objects found by archaeologists bear an increasing resemblance to the items we still use today. From nails, hinges, pins and needles, locks and keys to horseshoes, buckles and bits of old

WHAT COUNTS AS 'TREASURE'?

Examples of what is defined as 'treasure' in UK law:

- Any group of two or more prehistoric metals
- Precious metals (gold or silver) over 300 years old
- Any metallic object, or two or more coins, over 300 years old and with over 10% by weight precious metal
- Any other object found in the same place as the treasure

NOTE: it is your responsibility to research the latest government guidelines, and read the full up-to-date list at www.finds.org

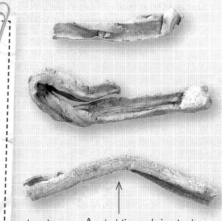

Lead cames for holding stained glass windows in place, Post-Medieval

Bronze tweezers, Roman or Early Medieval

Iron horseshoe, 16th–18th century

Bronze buckle from a sword-belt, 16th century

bicycles, you can have a great deal of fun just identifying what something is!

Iron is extremely prone to corrosion, but be wary of assuming that more corroded items are necessarily older. Multiple factors contribute to the rate of corrosion, chief among them the burial conditions. And as ever, be on the lookout for changes in colour and texture while you dig: sometimes all that remains of iron nails are reddish stains in the soil.

Hallmarks
The use of hallmarks (stamps to certify genuine gold, silver, etc) increased greatly during the industrial era, and they are particularly useful clues to the date and origin of a find. The Assay Office provides a good introduction to hallmarks: https://theassayoffice.com/anatomy-of-a-hallmark

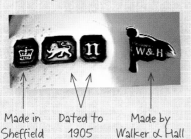

Made in Sheffield   Dated to 1905   Made by Walker & Hall

IDENTIFYING METALS
Metals make up a large part of the Periodic Table, but only a handful were isolated and used before the 19th century. Metals can also be combined to form alloys such as bronze and steel.

Metals

From c.2400 BC	Gold	Dense, malleable, bright reddish-yellow, corrosion-resistant
	Copper	Soft, malleable, yellow-orange, green corrosion product
From c.2000 BC	Tin	Soft, malleable, reflective, faint yellowish tinge
From c.800 BC	Iron	Soft, Grey, orange corrosion product
	Lead	Very dense, soft, malleable, silvery-grey on a fresh break, tarnishes to dull white-grey. Toxic.
	Silver	Soft, Malleable, silvery-white, tarnishes to black

Alloys

From c.2000 BC	Bronze	Copper + Tin	Range of colours, typically golden-brown, green surface corrosion common
From c.800 BC/ AD 1861	Steel	Iron + Carbon	Hard, silvery-grey Stainless steel (from 1861) is corrosion-resistant
From c.AD 43	Brass	Copper + zinc	Bright golden, corrosion-resistant
	Pewter	Tin + LEAD	Malleable, Silvery-bluish

Iron nail, Medieval

EXCAVATING FINDS AND FEATURES

Archaeological excavation is essentially a form of reverse engineering, in which we try to work backwards to discover the sequence of events that led to the formation of a site.

The fundamental principle of modern excavation is:

> *Take out the most recent thing first.*

Now, this is all very well when you have just de-turfed and you're looking at a nice patch of topsoil, but as you dig down, things tend to become more complicated. That's why archaeologists have developed a whole set of concepts and methods to help us understand what we're seeing, and to dig it all in the correct order.

STRATIGRAPHY

The *stratigraphic sequence* is the order in which archaeological contexts were formed, and it's what we're trying to unravel as we dig. Stratigraphy is concerned primarily with what happened before what, and can't give a precise idea of how long passed between various events.

The interface between the pinkish soil in the left of the trench, and the curved, darker brown soil

A moat was dug into the lighter-coloured soil, and later filled in with this darker material – the separation between the two is sharp and has structure (a curve), distinguishing it from the natural

CONTEXTS

A *context* is the smallest unit we can break things down to as we try to work out what order they happened in. Each context is given its own number, and any finds or samples from within it are labelled with that number, too. We assign context numbers to deposited layers of soil, and to features such as walls.

We also assign context numbers to processes that *remove* material, so long as they can be detected by the archaeologist. How can we detect the event of somebody removing soil to dig a ditch or a moat, for example? The answer lies in the sharp change in soil between the older ground surface that was cut into, and whatever material eventually filled it in. That line where the two different soils meet is known as the 'cut', and it, too, gets a context number.

THE MATRIX

The *matrix* (also known as the 'Harris Matrix', after its inventor) is a clever tool that visually represents the sequence in which contexts were formed. These relationships are mapped on a tree-like diagram that can be built up in your notebook as you dig. The top of the tree is the most recent event.

Let's say you've just finished removing the turf, and you're about to start digging the topsoil, which you label '(01)'. As you dig, any finds in the topsoil go into a finds tray with a '(01)' label. Now you come down onto a layer of different soil, so you label it '(02)' and start a new finds tray for anything that comes out. (01) lies over the top of (02), so it must be later in our stratigraphic sequence, and therefore at the top of the tree:

$$(01)$$
$$|$$
$$(02)$$

There is more detail on how to build up a matrix on page 196, but the key thing to bear in mind is that you must only draw lines between two contexts if there is a direct *stratigraphic* relationship between them. You may have two pits, and one is filled with Victorian finds, while the other one is full of medieval ones, but you can *only* draw a line between them if there is stratigraphic evidence for which came first, such as one pit partially cutting into the other one.

Hugh and Tash scrape back hard, exposing the raw surface of different contexts present

LEARN THE MOVES

'Enough with the theory,' I hear you cry (in chorus with every undergraduate university student I have taught these past fifteen years): 'We want to dig!'

Alright, alright. Let's get started by taking a look at some of the key moves the excavator has in their arsenal, starting with most important move of all, which is ... drum roll, please ... cleaning.

It may sound anticlimactic, but **cleaning** is one of the ways we see the archaeology. Cleaning is done to expose a fresh surface within the trench. This will help you to see (and feel) any soil changes, and will ensure that you don't accidentally contaminate a lower layer with finds from above.

When cleaning to expose a layer, get a firm grip on your trowel's handle, and scrape the soil towards you with the long, flat edge. Always work backwards and avoid stepping on any parts you've already cleaned.

Another piece of canny trowel-work you should be aware of is tracing the line of a cut. When you are **removing a fill** (for example, from

Cleaning the sides of the trench

If a find pops out during cleaning and you're not sure which context it belongs to, keep it separate and label 'unstratified'

a pit or post-hole), the aim is to take out all the material that filled the pit, but none of the stuff the pit was cut into. That way, you will be left with the exact shape of the original pit!

Bigger tools such as spades can be used when you are confident that you're working with an extensive deposit, but when in doubt, always stop, whip out your trowel, and have a bit of a clean! It also helps to take a step back and take in a wider perspective.

A half-section of an early medieval pit

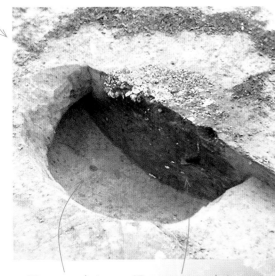

The excavated portion shows the original shape of the pit

The non-excavated portion, with the dark fill of the pit still visible

SECTIONING OFF AN AREA

One strategy often used by archaeologists is to focus time and resources on a smaller area of soil by creating a mini 'trench within a trench'.

There are lots of potential reasons for doing this:

- **Exploration:** the stratigraphy is complex and we're not sure which thing happened first. We take out a section of it to help us work out which order we should dig the rest in.
- **Efficiency:** we have little time remaining so we select the area of greatest interest and take it down further.
- **Safety:** when digging in deeper deposits, we might 'step' the trench by dividing it up and only digging further in one part of it.
- **Half-section:** when taking out the fill of a small 'negative feature' such as a pit or post-hole, we run a string between two nails to bisect it, and only remove half of the fill. This allows us to make a section drawing of the feature (see page 199).

9 POVERTY AND REDEMPTION

OSWESTRY

'I think it's a dark time in our history, really… it's not as ideal as it is today, that's for sure,' said Peter, a resident of Oswestry, in the English county of Shropshire, and just five miles east of the Welsh border. We were here because these peaceful streets and quiet cul-de-sacs concealed the buried remains of an enormous workhouse complex; once a last, desperate resort for paupers, orphans, and the uncared-for elderly in 19th-century Britain.

In 1723, the British Government passed the Workhouse Test Act, which stated that in order to access poor relief, people had to enter a so-called workhouse and undertake a set amount of labour. Developed in order to prevent fraudulent claims to poor relief, a crucial part of the idea behind the new legislation was that people should be deterred from choosing to go to a workhouse by making them as miserable a proposition as possible.

I think it's fair to say that they achieved this last aim, at least in the popular imagination. Thanks to the writings of Charles Dickens, the institution of the

The old isolation hospital – along with Morda Hall, one of just two of the surviving workhouse buildings

workhouse today is all but synonymous with gruel, cruelty and corruption. Yet there were over 500 workhouses in 19th-century Britain, and we were sure there must have been huge variation in how they were experienced by the inmates.

Built between 1792 and 1794, the Morda House of Industry on the outskirts of Oswestry was among the largest workhouses in the country, with an original capacity of up to 600 inmates, and ending up with 1,000.

The vast building complex underwent various modifications and expansions throughout the 19th century, including in 1891 the construction of the isolation hospital, one of the only parts to have survived to this day.

In the early 20th century, the workhouse became a welfare home – what at the time would have been termed a mental hospital or asylum. Always known simply as Morda House to the locals, the buildings survived until the early 1980s, when almost the entire site was destroyed by fire.

There was a real air of sadness in people when asked about the history of this place. 'I think the conditions in the workhouse were pretty grim,' said local resident Mo, who lives in a converted barn to the west of the

The enduring image of Victorian workhouses: Oliver Twist, asking for more gruel

workhouse, 'so it's probably got quite a sad history.'

Mo's neighbour Edward had his own connection with the history of the place, as his father's great-uncle had been a resident of Morda House. Half-remembered stories told by his elder relatives spoke of labyrinthine corridors and numerous inmates.

'It wasn't very nice, sometimes,' Edward concluded.

There were also local rumours about human remains turning up in the area. When the present-day housing estate was built here in the late 20th century, the bones of between 15 and 25 individuals were recovered, so we had to stay alert to the possibility of finding more while digging here. Most paupers would have been buried in unmarked graves, and mass graves were common, with up to 20–30 bodies being interred together.

The bones that had been recovered during building were eventually re-buried together in the present-day cemetery, and today an elegant plaque serves to remind the world of these lost, nameless souls.

HERE IN THE ARMS OF THE LORD
IS THE FINAL RESTING PLACE OF
THOSE FIRST BURIED AT
THE OLD WORKHOUSE
(ST. ANN'S CHURCH), MORDA
BETWEEN 1813–1856
MAY THEY REST IN PEACE
RE-INTERRED DECEMBER 19TH 2001
AND JANUARY 11TH 2002

As harrowing as it is to investigate the history of poverty, I believe it can also be redemptive. The human spirit is capable of incredible things, and as difficult as life

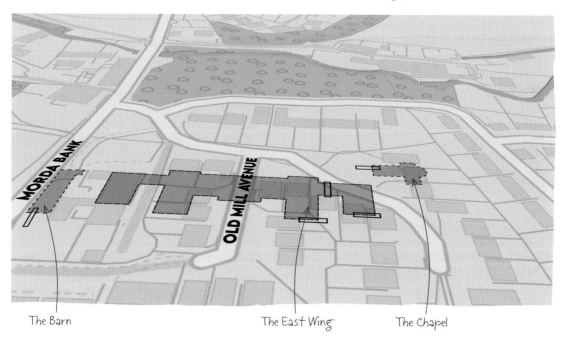

MORDA BANK

OLD MILL AVENUE

The Barn   The East Wing   The Chapel

must have been for Morda's inmates, they too deserve to have their story told.

I also found myself hoping that by coming here, we would be able to give the residents some peace of mind about the history of the place in which they lived. Happily for us, the locals were enthusiastic about the prospect of uncovering the history of the area in spite of its sad connotations, and our door-knocking had left us with several brilliant offers of help.

Social historian Dr Michala Hulme arrives in Dig HQ

While we drummed up some support, our experts were busy setting up in Dig HQ. As well as *Great British Dig* stalwart Dr David Griffiths, we were joined by our social historian Dr Michala Hulme, and leading expert on Victorian workhouses and children's homes, Peter Higginbotham. Peter first became interested in the institution of the workhouse after

discovering that his great-great-grandfather had died in one, and has spent over 20 years building up a meticulously researched database online, covering historical evidence for both workhouses and children's homes.

Back outside, Tash joined expert archaeologist Robin and local residents Claire and Peter to dig in the search of evidence of

Local resident and avid gym bunny Tyrik offered to help us dig... as long as it was in somebody else's garden!

the workhouse chapel, which historical records tell us was built in 1884. I was working with local lad Tyrik, who didn't think his mum would let us dig in their garden, but who was keen to help out nonetheless.

Almost as soon as we had opened a test pit in the garden of a willing neighbour, Tyrik made an interesting discovery. Finds of clay pipe stems are not uncommon on *The Great British Dig*, but this was the first time we had unearthed a fragment that included the mouthpiece!

'That's alright!' said Tyrik, smiling fondly at his find.

Tash left the chapel trench in Robin's trusty hands for a while to join Mo and Phil, the occupants of an old barn just to the west of where the workhouse stood. Mo had been

Leading workhouse expert, Peter Higginbotham

drawn to the building by its history, and although it had undergone extensive work to convert it into the charming house that stands there today, we hoped that evidence for its earlier function might still lie beneath the walled garden. Was this historic farm part of the workhouse complex?

Meanwhile, I did a bit of trench-hopping myself, and went to visit Anna and Gary's garden, where expert archaeologist Nathan was already working on our small test pit. This garden was located in what had

Breaking ground

What might the presence of clay pipe stems tell us about the workhouse?

Mo and Phil's converted barn when they first bought it...

... and today

been the East Wing of Morda House, close to the isolation hospital. As workhouses came under increasing pressure to pack in more and more inmates, so deadly diseases of the time – including cholera, tuberculosis and smallpox – flourished. The new isolation hospital would have allowed sick inmates to be treated without them risking the health of the entire workhouse population.

We hadn't dug very far before we happened upon a substantial water pipe. This was a classic Victorian piece of plumbing, meaning that it was a later addition to the original 18th-century design. It seems that, like the construction of the isolation hospital, we had hit upon evidence of improvements to the sanitation of the workhouse over time, that would have had great positive impacts on the health of its inmates.

A crowded London workhouse in the late 19th century

The slate pencil from Anna and Gary's trench

Anna and Gary discover the source of the mysterious trickling sounds under their lawn

Anna and Gary's trench had one more surprise in store for us, and I have to confess that it was my favourite. Digging away quietly by myself, I came across the sharpened tip of a slate pencil. Slate pencils were used by school pupils to practice their handwriting and arithmetic, and it is likely that this would have been a personal item, belonging to one of the children in the workhouse.

The Poor Law Amendment Act of 1834 obliged workhouses to provide at least three hours of schooling per day. As Michala explained to Hugh and David, although it included basic reading, writing and arithmetic, much of the workhouse training would have been vocational. For girls, this would have prepared them to find jobs in service, for example as maids; whereas boys were more likely to have received instruction in farming and manual labour.

I wasn't sure how to feel about this: glad, that the workhouse provided opportunities for future employment, or sad, that there was so little choice as to what this might be. And all the time, there was just *something* about the carefully sharpened tip of that slate pencil. It spoke to me of a child who had truly treasured this possession, perhaps because it represented a route out of the workhouse, and out of poverty.

I have to confess that I sometimes get a bit jealous of Hugh when he saunters off to fire crossbows, cook hearty medieval

Llanfyllin workhouse

stews, or tell tales around the hearth in reconstructed roundhouses, usually just at the point in the week when the digging gets tough. This time, however, he may have met his match in mild-mannered workhouse expert Peter Higginbotham, who had him breaking stones for his breakfast in order to experience one of the ways in which workhouses were made deliberately less attractive to the 'able-bodied, idle poor'.

But how did our star presenter get to this point? It started out when Peter took Hugh on a tour of the former workhouse of Llanfyllin in Montgomeryshire. Built 44 years after Morda in 1838, what we know of Llanfyllin is perhaps closer to the grim institutions of popular imagination. Records tell of

Vagrant men had to break stones to earn their breakfast

THE "SORTING" OF PAUPERS.

STONE-BREAKER'S CELL.

the schoolmaster being pulled up for using a leather strap instead of a birch rod to cane the children, while the children's guardians were investigated for putting four or five bed-wetters into the same bed.

As Peter explained, there was a lot of bed-wetting, because the children would be separated from their mothers on arrival. For me this sad little fact, born of such collective misery, brings home the stark reality of the workhouse far more than any caricature by Dickens, or the writers of musicals based on his works. Frightened children being taken from their mothers, for the crime of being poor.

Was life at the Morda House of Industry as bad as it seems to

Peter – whose name, after all, means 'stone' – breaks the news of his task to Hugh

Richard finds a cobbled surface by the barn

have been at Llanfyllin? I kept thinking of that little slate pencil, and wondering what sort of future its young owner could have looked forward to. Perhaps Tash could help us to find some answers as she called David over to check out the finds she had from within the Chapel.

They were certainly illuminating. A large fragment of worked stone from a window or doorway, some decorative painted wall-plaster, and even a lead *came* used to hold stained glass windows in place, all attested to a significant investment in this chapel, over and above what would have been required of your typical workhouse.

Meanwhile, Richard had discovered a substantial cobbled surface in Mo and Phil's garden, suggesting the presence of large farm animals, probably cattle. This was a bigger deal than it might sound. Richard's cobbles demonstrated that our missing building was not a farmhouse, but another barn. A series of barns with no associated farmhouse could

This large chunk of worked stone would have graced the door or windows of the chapel

only mean one thing: the farm belonged to the workhouse.

Farming was another activity that would have required hard physical labour, but it may have provided the inmates at Morda with a slightly better diet than the one enjoyed by those in urban workhouses, not to mention farming skills that could help them to get jobs on the outside.

Peter's flyer advertised a theatrical performance designed to raise funds to buy musical instruments for the boys' band

This fragment of pottery was almost an exact match for the example Peter had brought with him

Fire bricks are evidence for the installation of heating systems within the workhouse buildings

their porridge and gruel from. Clay pipe fragments, it turns out, were everywhere, suggesting that some little luxuries were allowed the inmates. Perhaps most amazingly, fire bricks – speciality bricks made to withstand high temperatures – attested to the installation of an indoor heating system at Morda.

To cap it all off, Peter did some digging of his own in the historical archives, and turned up with a flyer from the 1880s, advertising a theatrical performance designed to raise funds for a boys' band. Taken with Tash's findings in the chapel, and Richard's evidence from the barn, we were building a picture of workhouse life that changed for the better as time went by.

The 19th-century idea that poverty stemmed from a lack of moral rectitude may be at odds with modern sentiments, but

From this point on, Dig HQ was inundated with fascinating finds that shed light on daily life as a workhouse inmate. We brought in fragments of medicine bottles, ink bottles and pieces of the regulation pottery that the inmates would have eaten

Tash finds a fragment from a medicine bottle

The neck of an ink bottle

the religious beliefs of the 19th century also offered hope. Our investigation had thrown up multiple signs that the people running Morda House genuinely believed in the potential for reform, and it was this belief that must have driven the improvements made to it over time. Investment in the chapel, evidence for heating systems, better sanitation and medical care, some prospect of fresh food, little luxuries such as tobacco and music, and signs of education all attest to genuine attempts to improve the lives of the people who wound up here, and to help them find work on the outside.

I feel that in some way, we were also able to offer some redemption, in our case to the reputation of the Morda House of Industry amongst today's residents. Nobody wanted to wind up in the workhouse, but if you were to find yourself in such a place, you could do a lot worse than this one in Oswestry, Shropshire.

'We've learnt that it wasn't such a bad place - it wasn't the worst workhouse'

Clay Pipes

An example of a late 19th century, highly impractical decorative pipe

Tobacco was first introduced to the UK from the Americas in the 16th century. Clay tobacco pipes are one of the most common post-medieval finds on archaeological sites across the country. They were convenient, relatively easy to manufacture and seen as disposable; in other words, highly likely to show up at an archaeological site.

It is extremely rare to find a complete pipe, but luckily even fragments can provide a huge amount of information.

Bowl where the tobacco is packed and lit

Stem

Tip or mouthpiece

Spur or heel to help the pipe rest

Dating clay pipes

Pipes were made across Britain so expect some regional variation in what you might find, but there are some broad stylistic changes over time that can help with dating. The most useful parts of the pipe for dating are typically the bowl and heel/spur. Pipes with a wide heel or spur tend to date to the 16th and 17th centuries, whereas a narrow heel is a feature of later models.

Don't despair if you only find fragments of pipe stems. Here, too, there are some hints you can use for dating. The bore (the hole down the centre of the stem) tends to be wider in earlier clay pipes and narrower in the 18th and 19th centuries. The type of clay used also changed over time. Earlier pipes have a coarse fabric, occasionally with a mottled colour and other bits of material incorporated into the clay, but from around the late 18th century onwards, almost all pipes were made from high quality fine white clay.

16th century
The earliest clay pipes had small bowls, flat heels and straight, thick stems

17th century
As tobacco became cheaper, bowl sizes increased

Note how the angle and size of the bowl changes over time. The earliest pipes have smaller bowls, reflecting the rarity and thus expense of tobacco. The size increases as it becomes more available

Early 18th century
More upright bowls; tend to be more finely made

Late 18th century
The heel becomes a spur. Stems get thinner and the curved form is introduced

Sometimes, we are lucky enough to find decorated examples of both stems and bowls. Such specially-made exotic pipes with designs and markings can help us to tie down the date of the pipe, and even trace the company who manufactured it. The simplest example of this is a maker's stamp or mark, found on the stem or the base of the heel.

This example of a maker's mark on the pipe stem identifies the manufacturer as a Jonathan Lyon who made clay pipes in Birmingham in the early 19th century

A common form of decoration seen in the 19th century was the inclusion of shell-like or plant decoration around the bowl. This made the pipe more attractive and also provided a way to hide the mould lines from the manufacturing process

On this example, the maker's mark takes the form of a small flower on the spur

In the late 19th and early 20th centuries, the most common clay pipe form was the 'cutty'. These stocky pipes were more functional than elaborate, and they reduced in size by comparison with the ostentatious examples of the previous century

Formed mouthpieces to assist with holding the pipe between the teeth

Straight stem

DUBLIN

WANT TO KNOW MORE? There are many regional forms and typologies (diagrams that show the development of clay pipes over the centuries) that can be found on the internet. For those wishing to know more, the absolute best place to start is The National Pipe Archive at www.pipearchive.co.uk.

OUT ON THE GRANGE

BIGGIN HALL, COVENTRY

We met Hugh in the grounds of a cricket club to explain why we had been sent to Coventry – a line I sincerely hoped would be spoken by our star presenter himself, who has a habit of recycling my weak puns on camera, with ten times the stage presence I could ever muster.

Yet no matter how many times I threw it out, Hugh just wouldn't take the bait. To compound the insult, Tash told us she had never even heard the phrase. Just in case you, too, don't know what it means, to be 'sent to Coventry' is to be deliberately ignored and excluded: quite the opposite, in fact, of the warm welcome we received from the local community of Biggin Hall Crescent.

This was one of those occasions when the street names link directly to the archaeology beneath, because Biggin Hall was the later name of a building that had belonged to a medieval monastic grange. Granges were farms run by monks known as 'lay brothers', who worked the land

to supply food and other produce to their brethren, the 'choir monks', who mainly gave service through singing and prayer.

Some granges specialised in arable (crop) farming, others in cattle farming, or in sheep to supply Britain's growing wool industry. Some even included industrial complexes for craft production. While we didn't know which type this particular grange had been, we did know that it was built to supply the choir monks of St Mary's Priory, three miles to the west and founded in AD 1043. Later historical records tell us that after Henry VIII broke with the Catholic Church of Rome and dissolved England's monasteries from 1539, the land was sold off to the Draper's Company, a mercantile association who leased it out to farmers right through to the early 20th century.

As far as we were aware, almost all of the remains of the grange buildings were now buried beneath the later 20th century tarmac of Biggin Hall Crescent, so we weren't expecting to find any buildings remains in our residents' gardens. We had instead been drawn here by some intriguing 18th-century maps and more recent survey work, which suggested the medieval hall may have been surrounded by a moat on at least three of its sides. Would we be able

Lay brothers working the fields while the choir monks give service through prayer, mid–13th century

The standing remains
of St Mary's Priory

to find evidence for the moat on the other side, which now lies under the back gardens bordering the cricket club?

Moats are not your typical farm feature. Although some were defensive, they were also a physical reminder of social divisions between those on the inside and everybody else. The mystery of the moat was thus fundamental to our investigation. Was this a humble farm, barely eking out a living, or was it a grand site of industry, able to turn a profit and generate extra income for the Catholic Church at the height of its power in England?

There was, as ever, only one way to find out. As Hugh put it, 'All this means door-knocking.'

'That's why you're here,' quipped Tash with a grin,

Standing on the cricket pitch, Tash gestures in the direction of the back gardens that we hoped would contain evidence for a moat

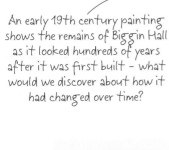

An early 19th century painting shows the remains of Biggin Hall as it looked hundreds of years after it was first built – what would we discover about how it had changed over time?

We located our trenches strategically to catch evidence for a possible moat associated with Biggin Hall

We hoped our trenches would pick up the missing side of the lost moat

The location of the hall, based on 18th century historical evidence

The moat, as suggested by historical survey

before bounding off to coax the locals into letting us do what we do.

We must have said something right, because the lovely locals were so welcoming that we were able to put trenches in three neighbouring gardens. Our projections of the buildings and moat – though not watertight – hinted that in one garden Tash, expert archaeologist Mandy and local resident Kieran might be able to catch a corner of the hall itself.

Tash was sure that if they could just get under the decking, they'd be certain to hit buried structures, but even her unique brand of

cheeky charm was not enough to convince a laughing Kieran, who deftly shifted the responsibility for saying 'no' onto her hubby, who was conveniently enough at work!

Meanwhile, Richard had inveigled himself

Tash and Kieran

John was hoping that the archaeologists might provide a spot of cheap labour for weeding and gardening, but he reckoned without the cost of their tea habits

into the garden next door, by sweet-talking retired couple John and Christine. John confessed he was expecting Richard to offer a bit of free weeding in exchange, but it turns out that Christine (who used to teach history in secondary school) was hoping he would uncover some evidence of scandal! Bit of a tall order, perhaps, but Richard is a tall bloke, so if anybody could deliver, it was him. Getting down to work with expert archaeologists Robin and Nathan, he bluffly replied that he'd see what he could do.

The residents of Biggin Hall Crescent were soon to discover that their local neighbourhood was not short of archaeological remains. From the moment our spades bit into the ground, the finds were coming up thick and fast. Working with expert archaeologist Marina, I encountered a beautiful example of a mid-20th-century find in a radio dial made of Bakelite, an early plastic.

I've always loved the fact that radio waves keep on travelling out into space, and I wondered when that radio was last tuned before it broke, and how far the waves from that day had travelled: 30, 40, 60 light years? Would any of them still be coherent if they were picked up by some alien device?

Marina, meanwhile, shook her head at me, and kept on digging.

The wavelength knob from a mid-20th-century radio

'How deep are you making this pond then, gardener?'

Mottled Ware

Richard looked a bit gutted

Next door, Richard and John had uncovered some fragments of Mottled Ware, a 17th-century pottery with a two-tone glaze and ridged design, perhaps belonging to the farm workers who leased the land out from the Drapers after it was sold off.

'Keep digging, then, let's get some more!' said John, before heading inside for a cuppa, presumably. Ever obliging, it wasn't long before Richard pulled out another exciting piece of pottery. He radioed finds specialist

Cistercian Ware

BELOW Don cores within Robin's trench to test how much deeper the deposits go, while Robin keeps a running tally of the measurements

CORING

The principle behind coring is simple: a slim tube of soil is extracted from the ground, allowing us to efficiently read the layers from top to bottom with a minimal amount of destruction to the archaeology. Coring is a specialist tool that is formidable when part of a larger kit, but it cannot tell us a huge amount without excavation and other forms of survey. Think of it as being akin to using a dipstick to check the oil in a car engine: it can tell you there is no oil present, but it can't tell you why.

A simple hand core, or 'auger', is essentially a large screw that is driven into the ground and turned, trapping the soil within its blades. The most basic technique requires multiple soil samples to be taken out and laid end to end, providing a top-to-bottom profile of what is under your feet. More elaborate cores can remove several metres of soil in one go, producing a tube of compacted soil that more closely resembles the buried sediments. For very deep or compacted sediments, percussion corers

ABOVE AND OPPOSITE
Examining the contents
of a core to detect the depth of various layers

Dr Hannah Russ, who confirmed that its 'gooseflesh' appearance and purple tinge identified it as Midlands Purple Ware. This late 14th- to 15th-century style was made for durability, and was probably being used to store the produce of the grange.

Any jealousy I may have felt over Richard's incredible haul of finds was soon tempered when I pulled out a beautiful jug handle identifiable by its dark, metallic glaze as a fragment of Cistercian Ware, a 15th- or 16th-century pottery type that was so named because it was once (incorrectly) thought to have been made by Cistercian monks.

'I like that,' said Richard distractedly. 'In fact I like that better than anything I've found in my trench to be honest.' Naturally, it's ridiculous to be competitive over archaeology. What's there is there and what's not is not; all we can do is to dig and record it to the best of our abilities. But somehow in Coventry, Richard and I forgot this: between his trench and mine, the gauntlet had been thrown down.

While we had been racking up the finds and bickering over who had the best trench, Don was hopping from one garden to another with his trusty hand core. He needed to sample the soil to search for silty sediments. Over time, the presence of water courses leads to silt formation, so by comparing those cores that brought up a silt layer with those that did not, he hoped to plot the location and depth of the buried moat.

Hannah was starting to notice some interesting patterns in the finds she was getting up at Dig HQ, especially those from Kieran's garden. An unusually large number of them looked like the by-products of high-temperature crafts including glass, pottery and metal production. With little reason for such waste products to travel far beyond

and other fuel-driven devices can be used.

It is always best to take multiple samples in an area to avoid being misled by anomalous results, but strategies vary based on what questions we are asking. At Beningbrough, for example (see page 134), Kris Krawiec took a straight line of closely-spaced cores cutting across a feature we spotted on the LiDAR imagery, allowing her to discover its 'profile' (shape) and depth. At both West Derby (see page 116) and Biggin Hall, we needed to cover a wide area to see whether we could pick up on evidence for moats, so rather than a single straight line, Don took cores from several points around the site.

SLAGS AND WASTERS

Wasters and slags are the by-products of pyrotechnology: the deliberate transformation of materials by raising them to extremely high temperatures. We can tell a huge amount about the tech behind ancient ceramics, metals and glass by the waste products left behind.

The most common by-products of **ceramic firing** are so-called wasters. These include ceramics that were heated too much and began to vitrify (turn

the site of manufacture, Hannah, Tash and I became increasingly convinced that the lay brothers at Biggin Hall were doing far more than working the land: it looked as though they were also making sophisticated craft products, which may have provided a significant boost to the grange's income.

Later, while I was back in my trench, I heard a curious rustling sound and

ABOVE Slags vary hugely in appearance but all have a slightly amorphous, glassy or spongy quality

RIGHT You won't find this on Etsy! Finds specialists Hannah and David added a festive message to this brick before sending it on its way for storage and conservation

BELOW The brick was so overheated at one end that it had begun to melt and flow

glassy and deform), ceramics with flaws in their fabric that meant they broke upon firing, or any kind of mistake involving glaze being applied to pottery and tiles.

Most **metals** used by humans do not naturally exist in isolation. They react with oxygen, carbonates and sulphides to form minerals that must be mined and then heated to extremely high temperatures in order to extract and work the metals, leaving a by-product known as 'slag'. Slags vary in appearance, but they are often dark or reddish in colour, and may appear glassy, spongy, or 'flowy'. The heavier the slag, the more metal it contains, indicating a less efficient extraction process. Vast amounts of slag were produced during the industrial revolution, and it was often transported

in bulk to be used as a rough construction material, but in earlier times the waste products usually stayed close to the site of manufacture.

More information can be found on the webpages of the Historical Metallurgy Society (www.historicalmetallury.org), which hosts the National Slag Collection (no sniggering at the back, thank you!).

Glass is a little more elusive. It does not leave any by-products such as slags, and you are less likely to find glass wasters because if a piece went wrong, it could easily be thrown back into the pot and recycled. If some hot glass or glaze dripped onto a dirty floor, however, or was spilt into the furnace and interacted with the fuel, it may have been too contaminated to recycle, becoming part of the archaeological record, instead – this is what I think we found at Biggin Hall.

Signs of an unexpected story began to show up in Kieran's garden

'Drip' of glass or glaze

A ceramic 'waster', or perhaps part of the kiln, this tell-tale fragment with glaze in all the wrong places is smoking gun evidence for craft production at Biggin Hall

A Peeping Rich

Evidence for the use of stone-working techniques to shape a brick is a reminder that early bricks were very high-status building materials

looked up to see Richard peering over the fence from his garden next door. He had been doing this intermittently ever since I found the Cistercian Ware. For once, I didn't mind the looming, because I had something rather exciting to show him.

I knew that Richard wasn't having much luck with finding his moat, and something equally perplexing was going on in my trench. Here, where we should have been outside the limits of the grange, I found what eventually showed itself to be the remains of a large, stone-footed wall. When this part of the grange was abandoned or destroyed, most of the more expensive stones would

have been taken and reused elsewhere, leaving just the foundation layer, and a scatter of the cobbles that made up the bulk of the wall in its centre.

No sooner had we identified the wall than we pulled out a beautiful piece of decorative brickwork from a door or window surround. This was late medieval brick, and it had been carved and ground into its final shape using labour-intensive stone-working techniques.

I originally thought this was a floor surface

After extending the trench, it was clear that it was part of a very substantial wall

people could afford to commission architectural elements such as these, suggesting that Biggin Hall was no low-budget grange.

It was starting to look like Biggin Hall had been larger and quite probably grander than we had realised, but why had we not seen any evidence of this in the later historical maps, or the painting? As it happens, our James thought he had the answer, and it came from among a layer of rubble in Richard's trench. He had identified a fragment of building stone that exhibited clear indications of having been cracked and deformed by extremely high temperature.

It was starting to look as though a part of the hall had burnt down at some

Not to be outdone, almost at the same time Richard's trench turned up a fragment of glazed floor tile. The skill involved in making these architectural elements rendered them very costly, and as everybody who has ever visited a DIY warehouse knows, once you scale up to cover an entire floor or wall, the price can skyrocket. Only the wealthiest

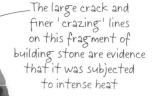

The large crack and finer 'crazing' lines on this fragment of building stone are evidence that it was subjected to intense heat

'If you get a stone hot enough, you can melt it!' enthused James to fellow softie Richard as they sat down for an archaeological teddy bear's picnic

point before it was recorded in the 19th-century painting and maps. And as for the moat, a combination of our excavation and Don's coring revealed that rather than encircling the grange and being designed to keep everybody else at bay, it had been a functional water course, diverted from the local stream, but leaving open access to Biggin Hall on one of its three sides. This particular grange, it seems, was both wealthier and more welcoming than had previously been assumed.

Another week, another fabulous adventure for the mad, travelling circus that is *The Great British Dig*. Much as I regretted having to move on from a site that had yielded so many incredible archaeological finds, at least I knew that the puns wouldn't be running out anytime soon. Sent to Coventry we may have been, but soon we were to be left to our own Devizes...

11 CRIME AND PUNISHMENT

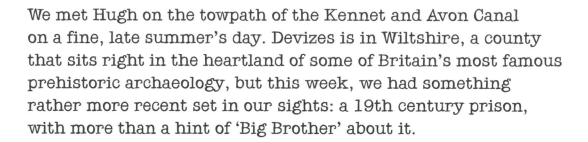

DEVIZES, WILTSHIRE

We met Hugh on the towpath of the Kennet and Avon Canal on a fine, late summer's day. Devizes is in Wiltshire, a county that sits right in the heartland of some of Britain's most famous prehistoric archaeology, but this week, we had something rather more recent set in our sights: a 19th century prison, with more than a hint of 'Big Brother' about it.

The 1960s houses and gardens sit right on top of the remains of a 19th-century prison, which we had reason to believe was built to a rather unusual design. The Devizes House of Corrections was built to a *panopticon* ('all-seeing') design. The concept of the panopticon had been developed by the English philosopher and social theorist Jeremy Bentham and his brother Samuel in 1785, and it was a sort of philosophical thought experiment made real.

Archaeologists Marina and Mandy arrive at work

'The guards' tower stood right here!'

A single guards' tower ringed by windows stood tall in the centre, with the cells blocks arranged around it. The idea behind the design was that, at any given moment, a prisoner would not know whether they were under surveillance or not, and would therefore be less likely to misbehave. This was architecture as a form of social control, and it was designed to change the way people thought as well as their behaviour.

When it was opened in 1817, Devizes House of Corrections was the only 'true' panopticon prison in the UK. With capacity for up to 700 prisoners but just 10 staff on the payroll, its unique design allowed a handful of guards to monitor and direct the lives of hundreds of prisoners. From our plans, we knew that the central guards' tower – which doubled up as the prison governor's house – stood somewhere on the Avon Road roundabout. Two hundred cells encircled it in a ring-shaped building, where today there are houses and gardens.

The building was demolished in 1927, and although we had a reasonable idea of

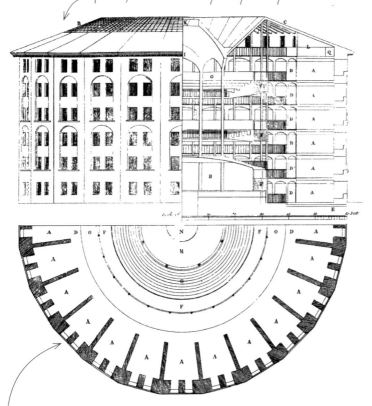

its overall appearance, we lacked detailed evidence on how it was built, the use of space within the prison, and the modes of surveillance employed by the guards.

Local resident Jo had warned us that we could dig in her garden as long as we didn't mind dogs, and although Richard had already called dibs on it, I wanted to hang out with some furry friends, so fellow archaeologist Nathan and I snuck in for a bit of cheeky de-turfing with Jo.

'We are so interested in the history of this place,' she told us. 'We were aware it was a prison before we moved in – my husband's a retired police officer, so we thought it was quite appropriate that we'd end up living in a prison!'

From the central tower, the guards could see into any cell, but the cells were separated from one another

The modern roundabout and street plan broadly follows the form of the prison

Jo stuns me with her enthusiasm for having us invade her garden!

It turns out that while they had been landscaping their beautiful terraced garden, Jo and her husband had found some hefty locks and chains from the prison. Leaving Nathan with strict instructions to find a set of chains, some iron window bars, a file, and a false moustache, I headed over to where fellow expert Alice was digging, in what we believed to have been the prison's gatehouse.

Meanwhile, Tash was putting her years of experience in commercial archaeology to good practice, by supervising the opening of

'Did somebody say BONE china?'

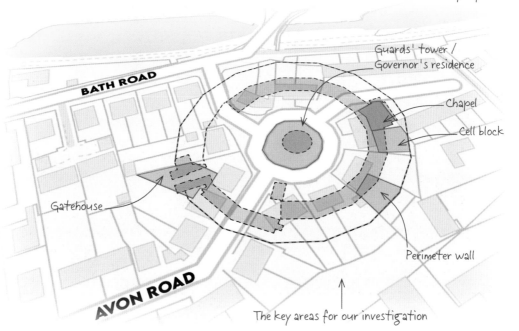

BATH ROAD

Guards' tower / Governor's residence

Chapel

Cell block

Gatehouse

Perimeter wall

AVON ROAD

The key areas for our investigation

Tash brings in some mechanical assistance for the big trench

a trench by digger on the central roundabout, right over where we believed the large guards' tower to have stood.

'Ironically, we're on a roundabout, which is also a circle,' she chirped. I can't be certain, Tash, but I suspect that might have been a deliberate choice on the part of the builders!

We hoped that Tash's trench would provide an interesting contrast to those located around the cellblocks, by providing glimpses of life inside the tower, and we were not to be disappointed. Tash soon called finds expert Hannah over to take a look at a curious piece of worked animal bone. Hannah identified this extraordinary find as an early example of a toothbrush handle, and by carefully cleaning off the dried soil she exposed a stamp that read 'Madgwick, Devizes' – a local chemist.

Back in Dig HQ, *The Great British Dig* regular and social historian Dr Michala Hulme offered yet more insight into the rare find. As she explained to Hugh, in the 19th century

This bone-handled toothbrush was bought from a local chemist

Expert archaeologist Marina takes out the topsoil

seemingly from the ether:

'Hello there, what are you doin' to my neighbour's garden?' It turns out that the source of this accusation was a grinning, friendly face that I soon learnt belonged to next door neighbour Jeremy, who was peeping over the fence. Once he found out what we were up to, he was keen to jump in and lend a hand and so, naturally, we co-opted him into carrying our spoil. You've got to start somewhere, people.

toothbrushes were luxury items reserved for the wealthier middle and upper classes, so it is likely that our toothbrush belonged to the governor or a member of his family. In case you were wondering, they didn't have toothpaste as we know it, but they were brushing their teeth with charcoal, which seems to have come back into fashion as a beauty ingredient recently.

Having joined Alice in the garden that we thought lay over the original prison gatehouse, I was suddenly startled by a voice,

I put Jeremy to work carrying spoil

As Jeremy heaved spoil, we chatted about the significance of the gatehouse as the point of entry – and departure – for prisoners. Upon first arriving, they would have been stripped and de-loused, before entering the main prison and first encountering the great, ever-watchful tower. And it was here, too, that people would have left the prison. Some of them would hopefully have gone on to start new lives, never to return the House of Corrections.

For others, however, that walk to the gatehouse would have been their last: until 1868, when public execution was banned, this was where prisoners were hanged, and sometimes where their bodies would remain hanging as they began to rot, a harsh reminder of the ultimate penalty for going against the law.

The estate was certainly not short on finds, and our local residents beat a well-trodden track between their gardens and Dig HQ over the course of the week.

'I'm actually holding something that somebody held years ago – probably a criminal,' said Jeremy gleefully, as he lifted the steel handle of a prison issue mug.

From the area of the guards' tower and governor's residence came finds hinting at a rather more luxurious existence, including hand-painted pottery and a large stone slab for keeping meat and cheese cool. Tash found a piece of rolled glass, probably to prevent prisoners from seeing into the governor's private rooms. Rather wonderfully, she also turned up an enormous metal file, throwing to mind the image of prisoners desperately trying to saw their way through the iron bars.

As we continued to dig, however, I struggled to imagine anybody managing to break out, given the sheer scale of the surviving prison architecture. In the garden of local resident Frank, we had uncovered some of the outer wall belonging to the cell blocks, up against which the prison chapel had later been built. Exposing this wall

Michala and Hugh discuss the finds

Tash picks Richard's brains over her finds

Rolled window glass

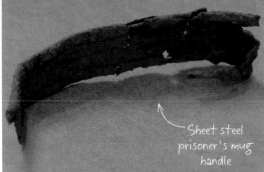

Sheet steel prisoner's mug handle

Victorian cut-throat razor

foundation gave us an incredible insight into the construction of the prison building: what must have been a great thickness of solid concrete – a little-used building material at the time – sealed off any potential weak spots between wall and floor, and with it, surely, any hopes of escape by tunnelling.

Tash was also experiencing emotional reactions to what she found, after her roundabout trench turned up some enormous metal hinges belonging to the prison doors. As she told Hugh, 'You can imagine when you're in a prison, you've got these massive doors, and the sounds they make when they close. That's what I get when I look at it: the feeling the inmates must have had when they heard that door slam.'

Later, during a visit to Dig HQ, I got chatting to local historian John Girvan, who has spent years collecting material on the

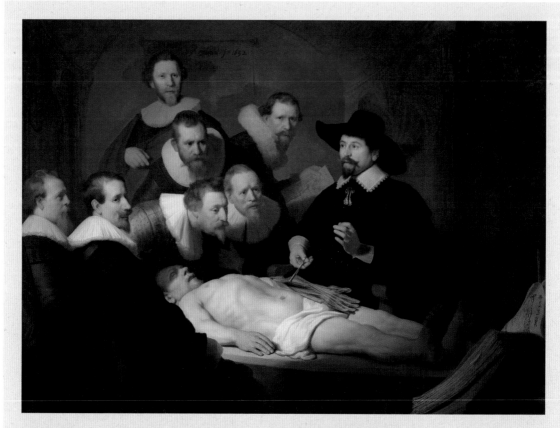

THE CRIMINAL CORPSE

In 2014 I was working as a researcher at the University of Leicester, on the top floor of a slightly run-down building set a little apart from the main campus. Among the eccentric charms of this workplace were a piano that only seemed to play when nobody was looking, and some kind of illicit squirrel activity in the attics. When any of us needed to scan a book, or make a photocopy, we were obliged to head downstairs to the first floor, and use the machine housed in the offices of another project.

Much as I adored the work I was doing, I couldn't help but be fascinated every time I had to hang about in the rooms belonging to Professor Sarah Tarlow's *Harnessing the Power of the Criminal Corpse* project. Old newspaper stories and grim woodcuts were pasted haphazardly to the walls, and I would read them in awestruck fascination as the copier whirred and clicked in the background. Professor Tarlow and her team were researching the history of what happened to the bodies of executed criminals after their death.

Criminal punishment in 18th and earlier 19th century Britain was a public affair. Physical punishments such as whipping and hanging took place in public spaces, but this desire for social humiliation was not limited to

RIGHT The 1701 gibbeting of William Kidd, near Tilbury in Essex, from a woodcut of 1837

OPPOSITE Public anatomy lesson as depicted by Rembrandt, 1632

the living. Even after death, the remains of executed criminals were seen as potent, as shown by the trade in criminal body parts for magic and medicine.

The 1752 Act for Better Preventing the Horrid Crime of Murder insisted upon the necessity for further deterrents, over and above execution, for the most grievous crimes of the day. After it was passed, judges were given the power to command that after death, the bodies of executed criminals were subject to further humiliation, either by 'gibbeting' (left on public display to rot, often in an iron cage), or by post-mortem dissection, often before an audience.

It is an uncomfortable truth that much of the medical knowledge we benefit from today was borne out of the dissection of individuals who had not given their consent. The bodies of criminals were sought-after by medical students keen to learn anatomy, but there would never be enough to satisfy demand, leading to the infamous practice of 'body snatching', whereby freshly-buried corpses would be dug up in secret and sold on for profit. This in turn led to the use of 'mortsafes'; iron cages that were placed around coffins to prevent grave-robbing.

Popular support for post-mortem punishment was never universal, and it waned greatly throughout the 19th century. Gibbeting was officially ended in 1834, although it had been declining in popularity for many years prior to this. Just two years before, the 1832 Anatomy Act had ended the use of dissection as a post-mortem punishment for executed criminals, but had at the same time legalised it for the *unclaimed bodies* of those who died in workhouses or jail.

LEFT A surviving mortsafe in Greyfriars Kirkyard, Edinburgh

John's photograph of the prison demolition, showing similar windowsills with their iron bar fittings still in place

complete, with a series of diamond-shaped holes in them. Behind these was a standing wall and clue to their purpose: they were windowsills, with specially cut spaces into which the enormous iron bars would have been firmly fitted.

There is something visceral about meeting the sheer impenetrability of these surviving fragments in person. No set of architect's plans can quite match the shock of your spade suddenly thwacking against a thick concrete floor, its metallic protest ringing back up your arms. No account of prison security can offer the sensation of losing your body heat through your hands as you press them into the cold, rough stone of a windowsill designed to hold

prison. Spotting me puzzling over a hefty chunk of stone architecture with an odd shape, John hurriedly disappeared, only to return a short while later with an album of photographs taken during the early 20th-century demolition of the prison.

There, in the foreground of one picture, were two very similar piece of stone, albeit

'This would be too big to bake into a cake!'

The large stone windowsill fragment we recovered from the roundabout

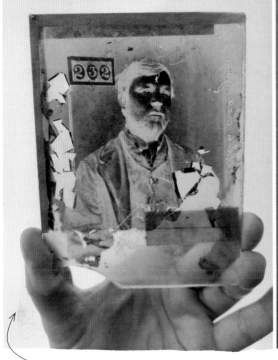

John provided us with one final, wonderful treasure from his collection: a series of photographic plates depicting prisoners, which had turned up some years before in a local garden

thick iron bars – and people – in their place.

As we had been digging away, digital archaeology expert Marcus Abbott was carefully documenting the structural findings within our trenches, and in particular, the large trench on the roundabout, where Tash was now finding evidence for a sunken walkway that the guards would have used to patrol the exercise yards unseen.

Back in Dig HQ, Marcus carefully pieced his data together to build a virtual reconstruction of the prison... with a twist! He hooked his mobile phone up to a VR viewer, creating a three-dimensional, immersive panopticon prison experience. Raising

his head, Hugh commented upon the stark prison buildings and hidden watchpoints, and how they contrasted with the pristine lawn and frosted upper windows of the governor's residence.

Hugh takes a virtual trip to jail

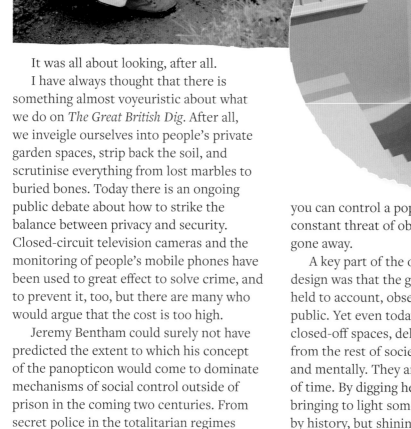

Tash's stairs were incorporated into Marcus's reconstruction model

It was all about looking, after all.

I have always thought that there is something almost voyeuristic about what we do on *The Great British Dig*. After all, we inveigle ourselves into people's private garden spaces, strip back the soil, and scrutinise everything from lost marbles to buried bones. Today there is an ongoing public debate about how to strike the balance between privacy and security. Closed-circuit television cameras and the monitoring of people's mobile phones have been used to great effect to solve crime, and to prevent it, too, but there are many who would argue that the cost is too high.

Jeremy Bentham could surely not have predicted the extent to which his concept of the panopticon would come to dominate mechanisms of social control outside of prison in the coming two centuries. From secret police in the totalitarian regimes of the 20th century, to the use of dummy speed cameras in the 21st, the idea that

you can control a population through the constant threat of observation has not gone away.

A key part of the original panopticon design was that the guards, too, should be held to account, observable by the general public. Yet even today, prisons remain closed-off spaces, deliberately kept apart from the rest of society both physically and mentally. They are places almost out of time. By digging here, we were not only bringing to light something all but forgotten by history, but shining our torches back on that guards' tower, and trespassing into a place that social norms usually seal off.

When it was my turn to put on the VR headset, and I stared up at the formidable, all-seeing monolith ahead of me, I almost experienced a sense of liberty rather than oppression: we had set the stories of these prisoners free.

A prisoner's approach: the first view a prisoner would have had on entering the prison from the gatehouse was of the imposing central guards' tower, as visualised by Marcus Abbott

Local residents come to Dig HQ to see the finds

RECORDING YOUR FINDINGS

Imagine that after you have finished excavating, you need to be able to reconstruct the layers and features in your trench from the bottom to the top. By making notes about what we see while we are still digging, we can understand the sequence of past events long after we've finished backfilling.

Recording strategies are decided before an excavation begins, and take into account loads of factors, but there are some general guidelines that pretty much always apply:

When should I record my findings? You will need to make a record every time you suspect you have hit a new layer or feature – any of the things we term together as a context (see page 151).

What should I record? Use plans and notes to record the spatial extent and depth of contexts, how they relate to one another *stratigraphically* (see page 150] and the section on soil composition on page 132), and their approximate location in the trench.

How should I record? There are a few different conventions out there. The most important thing is to be consistent, and to keep a combination of written notes along with plans and sections.

What if I go wrong? Only the most grievous of archaeological perjurers will pretend they have never made a mistake! Happily, with a proper recording system in place, you can compensate for most errors.

Fun fact: there is an entire sub-branch of archaeology dedicated to deciphering Robin's handwriting

Common Recording Conventions

Tr 01	trench number
#	charcoal flecks
下	level taken here
— ·· —	limit of excavation (e.g. trench edge)
(03)	deposit or fill number
07	cut number
[12]	structure number
·.::.	mortar flecks
— · — ·	edge of context
⟩⟩	hachures to represent slopes
⬆N	arrow pointing north

MATRIX

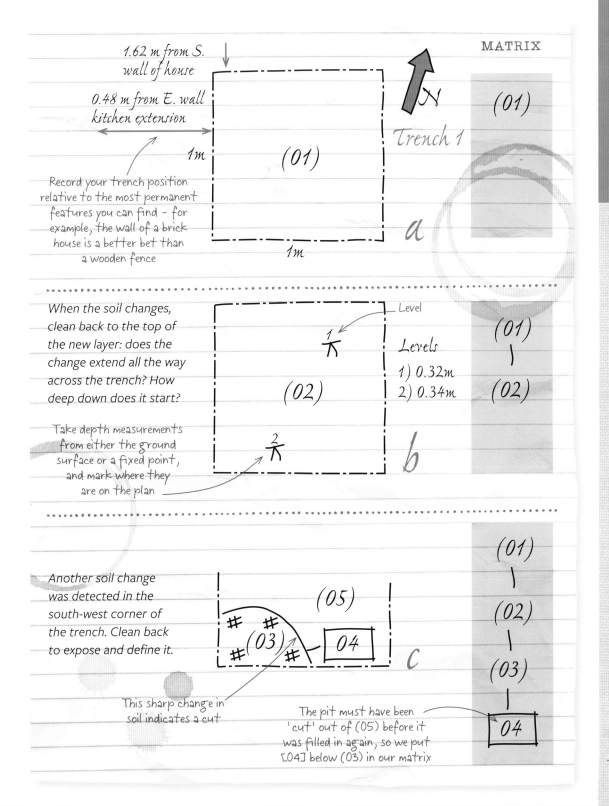

1.62 m from S. wall of house

0.48 m from E. wall kitchen extension

1m

N

Trench 1

(01)

(01)

a

1m

1m

Record your trench position relative to the most permanent features you can find – for example, the wall of a brick house is a better bet than a wooden fence

When the soil changes, clean back to the top of the new layer: does the change extend all the way across the trench? How deep down does it start?

Take depth measurements from either the ground surface or a fixed point, and mark where they are on the plan

Level

Levels
1) 0.32m
2) 0.34m

(02)

b

(01)
|
(02)

Another soil change was detected in the south-west corner of the trench. Clean back to expose and define it.

(05)

(03)

04

c

This sharp change in soil indicates a cut

The pit must have been 'cut' out of (05) before it was filled in again, so we put [04] below (03) in our matrix

(01)
|
(02)
|
(03)
|
04

MATRIX

(01)
|
(02)
|
[06]
|
[07]

A second feature was cut into the deposit (05), in the north-west of the trench

Can you detect anything filling the gap between the bricks and the original foundation cut? If so, this also needs a context number!

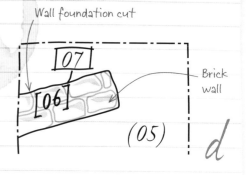

Wall foundation cut

[07]

[06]

Brick wall

(05)

d

. . . .

Let's bring together these new features on a single plan...

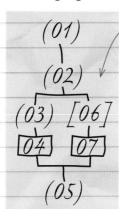

(01)
|
(02)
|
(03) [06]
[04]   [07]
|
(05)

There is no direct stratigraphic relationship between the pit and the wall, so they are on separate branches of the matrix. We don't know which came first, but they both dug into (05) so they must be later than it, and (02) lay over the top of them, so they must be earlier than it!

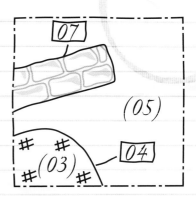

[07]

(05)

(03) # #   [04]

e

. . . .

What should you dig next?
Remember, we always take out the most recent context first. We don't know if the pit or the wall went first...

We didn't want to destroy the whole wall, so we just took out a section of it, to explore how it relates to the surrounding contexts

We took out the contents of the pit, and found that it sloped gently at the top, and sharply at the base

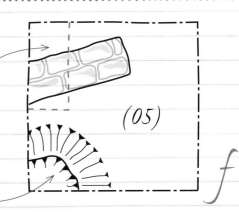

(05)

f

SECTION DRAWING

Once you have finished excavating, section drawings (i.e. of the side of the trench) are really handy for showing the depths of layers, checking against your plans, and spotting anything you might not have seen while digging. This part is definitely easier with an assistant!

1 Give a good solid clean to the section you want to record, and score out the lines between the contexts with the tip of your trowel.

2 Drive two nails into the ground at each end of the section you're drawing. Locate them a bit past the original corners, or they'll collapse into the trench!

3 Run a string between the two nails, a few inches above the topsoil and tie it nice and taut. If your ground surface is fairly flat, use it as a guide to keep the string from sloping up or down. Better yet, use a spirit level.

4 Let's start by drawing the surface of the topsoil. Measure from the left-hand nail – how far in from this does your trench start? How far down from the string is the surface of the topsoil?

5 Continue taking measurements at regular intervals, and use your eye to fill in the gaps.

6 Do the same thing to draw in the base of the topsoil (01), and so forth.

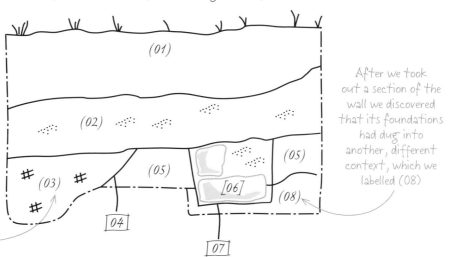

Trench 01, Post-Excavation, East-Facing Section, Scale 1:20"

This drawing was made of the westernmost section of the trench - the one that looks out towards the east ('east-facing')

(01)

(02)

(03)

(05)

(05)

[06]

(08)

[04]

[07]

After we took out a section of the wall we discovered that its foundations had dug into another, different context, which we labelled (08)

You can still see the contents of the pit in (03) where it ran into the side of the trench and we had to stop digging

The Great British Dig

199

ROYALISTS AND PARLIAMENTARIANS

KING'S LYNN, NORFOLK

It might seem peaceful now, but in the year 1643 the port town of King's Lynn, on the coast of The Wash in Norfolk, fell under siege, in an early stage of what would become known as the English Civil Wars. Fought over 7 years between the Royalists, who were loyal to the king, and the so-called Parliamentarians, loyal to Parliament, the Civil Wars were eventually to culminate in the execution of King Charles I, and the installation of Oliver Cromwell as Lord Protector of the new – albeit short-lived – republic.

King's Lynn had started out a Parliamentarian stronghold, but in 1643 its governor dealt an abrupt blow by switching allegiance to the Royalists. In one of the most critical moments of the English Civil Wars, Royalist forces on their way to secure possession of the town

were held up around the Humber, and the Parliamentarians were able to breach its walls and resume their access to its important trade routes with continental Europe. These trade links made King's Lynn the ideal supply base for Parliamentarian forces in the east of England and, unwilling to let it go again, they set about remodelling the defences that had fallen so easily to their own assault.

Throughout the medieval period, castle and town walls developed from the sort of earthwork and timber structures of motte and bailey castles (see page 116) to large stone buildings surrounded by thick, high walls and curving bases to protect them from being undermined. For centuries these remained state-of-the-art in defensive warfare, but now, times were changing.

Ever-imaginative when it comes to developing new ways to kill each other, people were increasingly making use of gunpowder, with all its devastating potential, and which could propel cannon balls to tear through medieval stone defences like a thumb through wet tissue.

We tend to assume that technological

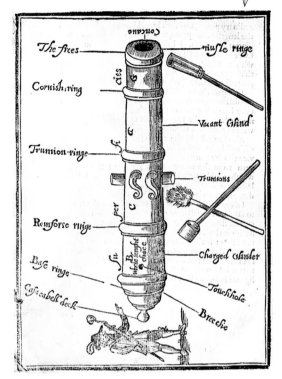

change moves in a single direction, but in this case, the solution to these new weapons was a return to an older technology: the use of monumental earthen defences that would simply suck in cannon balls rather than

buckling under their fire. In place of curved walls, the new design used a confusing series of angular forms such as bastion towers, and forced attackers to pass through a gruelling obstacle course of moats, dips, raised earth and hidden firing points.

And that's how we came to be here in King's Lynn, looking for the biggest thing we had yet tried to find on *The Great British Dig*.

'Up for a bit of door-knocking?' asked Hugh, breezily. 'Nobody's ever said no.'

'Not to you,' quipped Tash.

Perhaps wishing to steer clear of Tash's sharp wit, Hugh organised an investigative mission, with digital archaeology expert Marcus Abbott and military historian David Flintham, to seek historical evidence for the defences at King's Lynn. David leads the *King's Lynn Under Siege* project, and he brought a small army of volunteers to help us dig.

The group converged at the site of an unassuming duck

This duck pond originally belonged to the moat that stretched around King's Lynn as part of its 17th-century defences

The bastions would have allowed the defenders to fire in multiple directions

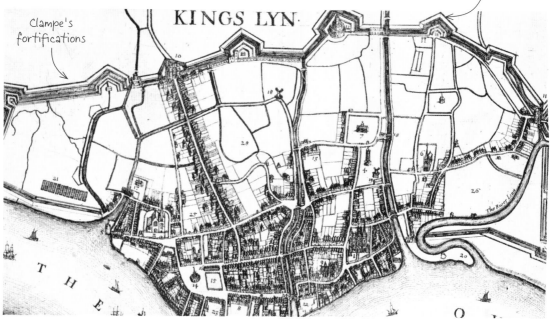

Clampe's fortifications

KINGS LYN

Today, the moat is home to a squabbling population of ducks, geese and swans

daunting. Even our hand-dug trenches were as long and thin as possible, to maximise our chances of hitting the features that cut across them. This would not have been enough, however, without the generous permission of local farmer and sea-swimming champion Steve and his family, who allowed us to use a digger to open a 30m trench in their freshly ploughed field. The aim here was to cut the trench as a cross-section through the defences, so that we could gauge how much the actual ground plan varied from the architect's drawing.

'We're looking for earthworks... in earth,' said Richard, with a bit of a wry grin, but Hugh was nonplussed.

pond, which it turns out was once a portion of the defensive moat, and examined an invaluable historical document that lay at the core of our investigations. It was the original plan for the defences, drawn up by physician and mathematician Richard Clampe, and it showed a series of enormous earthen mounds and ditches, with fancy bastions at the corners. As nobody had ever excavated the defences, however, we had no idea how much their builders had stuck to the original design, and no way of knowing what construction techniques were used to build them.

This was a different kind of archaeology for us on *The Great British Dig*, and the sheer scale of what we were trying to expose was

David Flintham

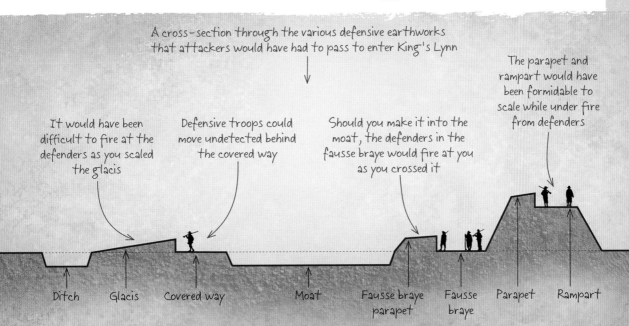

A cross-section through the various defensive earthworks that attackers would have had to pass to enter King's Lynn

It would have been difficult to fire at the defenders as you scaled the glacis

Defensive troops could move undetected behind the covered way

Should you make it into the moat, the defenders in the fausse braye would fire at you as you crossed it

The parapet and rampart would have been formidable to scale while under fire from defenders

Ditch   Glacis   Covered way   Moat   Fausse braye parapet   Fausse braye   Parapet   Rampart

The digger opens a 30m long trench in the hope of picking up a cross-section through the defences

'We're in a field...' began Richard

'The phrase always used to be, "It's like finding a needle in a haystack",' he replied, 'but you can do that now because of metal detectors. I've got absolute faith in you.'

The top layers of our trenches were a mixed bag in terms of finds, but – as our expert Hannah Russ pointed out to Hugh when he paid her a visit in Dig HQ – any 17th-century remains among them would be a good sign that we were looking in the right place. The layers of soil that build up in the ground over time never do so undisturbed:

the actions of roots, burrowing animals, and people ploughing or planting all serve to mix the soil, especially in the top few layers. That's how we end up with what are known

Brothers Zack and Arthur were brilliant at finding cool stuff!

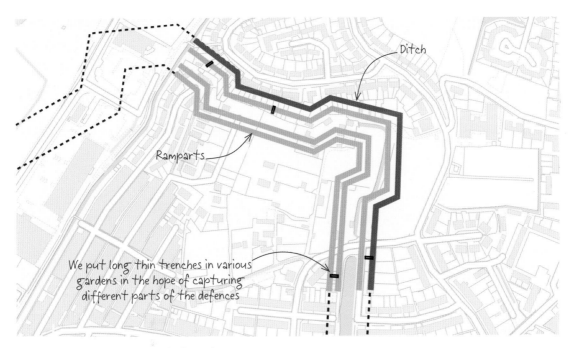

Ditch

Ramparts

We put long thin trenches in various gardens in the hope of capturing different parts of the defences

as 'residual' finds; materials from lower layers that find themselves in the topsoil, and signal to us that there may be richer seams of them lower down.

East Anglia is full of flint, which was great if you lived in the Stone Age, when – due to its predictable fracture pattern – flint was one of the main materials used for making tools. Because it was part of the natural geology of the area, we were finding loads of flint nodules and fragments of broken flint as we dug.

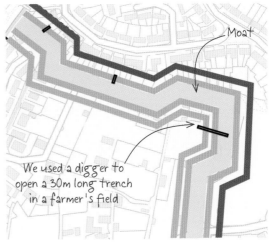

Moat

We used a digger to open a 30m long trench in a farmer's field

But in one family's garden I turned up a find that struck me to my core: a piece of flint with evidence for having been worked by humans. Along one of its edges was a line of what we call 'retouch', where somebody had carefully pressured off some flakes to sharpen their tool. The tool looked like a scraper, which would have been used to clean the fat from animal hides, and this – coupled with the way it had been worked – identified it as having belonged to the Mesolithic period; the 'Middle Stone Age', up to 12,000 years ago, when people in Britain were

Tash found some very recent archaeology, in the form of a Furby

The characteristic marks on this stone tool date it to the Middle Stone Age, and our expert's analysis suggests it was about 10,000 years old

The little chips at the edge of this piece of flint were made deliberately to sharpen its edge

hunter-gatherers who led a largely nomadic lifestyle.

The flint was what we would term 'residual' and was mixed in with 18th- and 19th-century finds – also residual – but it was nonetheless hugely exciting, and the oldest archaeological find we have made to date on *The Great British Dig*.

Hannah had been asked to leave Dig HQ for a bit and pop over to the long trench in Steve's field, to identify a piece of pottery that Richard suspected might be of the right date. She immediately recognised it as Red Ware, a type of 17th-century pottery that was made locally in imitation of more expensive Dutch imports.

Having left a happy Richard to carry on digging, Hannah was diverted on her way back to Dig HQ by a call from Tash, who had been digging at one end of the large

trench, and needed her expert advice on some animal bones. Hannah confirmed Tash's suspicions that they had belonged to a dog, but noted that it was most likely quite a bit later than the Civil War period.

She was able to deduce this because the dog's skull was small, but contained all of its adult teeth, confirming that it was not a puppy and thus would have belonged to one of the more fancy dog breeds that did not emerge until relatively recently.

Next on Dr Hannah Russ's Grand Finds ID Tour was the trench I was digging with expert archaeologist Alice, in Derek's front garden. Here, we were hoping to find evidence of the glacis and perhaps the outer, water-filled ditch of the defences... but we had instead turned up a whole series of curious little pits, filled with strange spiky

Hannah identifies a fragment of 17th-century Red Ware in Richard's trench

bones that I suspected belonged to fish.

Frankly, these bones creeped me out a bit, and I wanted to know what animal they came from and why there were so many of them. Hannah was nothing short of ecstatic as she sifted through the finds tray, and I was reminded of my son opening his stocking on a Christmas morning.

'Ooh,' she enthused, 'I've never seen them as well-preserved as these. These are spikes of the Thornback Ray, which is more closely related to sharks.' Hannah explained that because most the bones in these fish were cartilaginous (and thus more susceptible to

Hannah and Richard chat pottery finds in the big trench

degradation) it is extremely rare to find them in archaeological contexts. She was even more excited to discover a jawbone among our finds, as these were rarer still.

I eventually cast aside my suspicions that Derek had a secret Thornback Ray habit, as the other finds from this trench showed that the pits belonged to the late 19th or early 20th century, telling us a story of later life in this port town. Incidentally, the credit for this trench must also be shared by Derek's granddaughter Isobel, who spent every moment she could sifting through our spoil heap, picking out any tiny finds we had missed while digging with her keen eyes and her borrowed, oversized trowel.

Alice and Isobel working together in Derek's front garden

Any fears that we were not finding enough 17th-century material were allayed by Tash, who had an exciting find in the form of another fragment of chert, a fine-grained material with similar properties to flint. This was no Mesolithic tool, however, but a 'gun flint', distinguished from prehistoric stone tools by its neat squared-off edges.

Animal bones expert Dr Hannah Russ really had her work cut out for her this week

Tash finds a dog skull

Small dog breeds were not common until the Georgian and Victorian periods

Home-owner Derek discovers that his garden is home to a cache of Thornback Ray bones

Fish bone expert Hannah was thoroughly delighted with our Thornback Ray

We collected tray after tray of these unusual bony specimens

Gun flints such as this were used from the 17th to the mid-19th century. They were a crucial part of firearms technology, as they were struck against a piece of steel, creating the spark that ignited the gunpowder and discharged the shot.

Later that day, as we sat down to eat, I noticed a rather despondent Hugh Dennis shuffling over to rifle dejectedly through the sandwich options. He seemed to be nursing a bruise on his head, and muttering something that sounded like 'shoddy helmets.'

As it turns out, he had been off to meet some Royalist and Parliamentarian reenactors, including two chaps dressed in almost identical garb, who in fact represented soldiers on opposing sides. This didn't seem to fit with anybody's preconceptions of the Royalist 'Cavaliers' or the Parliamentarian 'Roundheads' as they used to be known, but historian and weapons

expert Jo Sonex was on hand to explain that while there was some difference between the two sides in the way officers dressed, ordinary soldiers would have had to distinguish their allegiance on the battlefield by wearing a particular colour or piece of greenery they found on the day.

Anyway, after explaining all this to Hugh, they swiftly rammed a helmet on his

Tash found a chert gun flint

unmistakable remains of massive timber stakes that had been driven into the soil.

It appears that the earthen ramparts had been constructed around a sturdy timber framework, which would have provided support and stability to the high defences and explains how it was possible to build them to such an enormous scale. David and his volunteers were delighted. As he put it, 'we know more about how the Romans built their fortresses than the fortresses of the Civil War.'

Elsewhere along the length of their enormous trench, the team had found evidence for what had once been the moat. This, too, was recognised by characteristic changes in the soil: darker, looser soil and silt where

Which is the Roundhead, and which the Cavalier?

head and clonked him pretty heavily and unexpectedly with a sword, presumably the cause of his later head-rubbing and the muttering. They did redeem themselves slightly by letting him hold a massive pike and make a *Dad's Army* pun, so at least he got a joke out of it.

Back in the field, Richard had struck gold… or, more truthfully, a slightly different-coloured soil. He was delighted, though, because this is exactly what we had been looking for. Characteristic dark stains with neat, straight-edged outlines were the

'Don't tell 'em your name, Pike!'

Richard considers the evidence for defences in the large trench

'I think it's very much of national importance,' said David

Progress is made in the large trench

the moat had eventually become filled in, with a sharp edge where it had been cut into the more compacted soil that still remained below and on either side of it. The moat was far wider than had originally been assumed based on Clampe's plan: 20m rather than 15m, which would have made the defences even more difficult to breach.

I must confess, I had always had my doubts about Clampe's plan. After all, it's easy enough to draw an enormous earthwork from the comfort of your nice little townhouse, but how did we know that the people on the ground didn't cut corners, or – perhaps more kindly – adapt his plans to accommodate the lie of the land?

The discovery that the moat was in fact wider than expected fed into my suspicions, although its extended size slightly disabused me of the notion of sloppy workers trying to get away with less work! But I was blown away by Richard's next discovery.

He had discovered that the inner line of the moat, including the fausse braye and the principal rampart behind it were preserved to a remarkable degree, with the

Richard tells David about his findings in the big trench

The rotted remains of timbers leave a dark, regular stain in the earth

original lines where they had been cut into the ground remaining crisp and clear to this day. When compared with Clampe's original plan, we discovered that every one of the architect's measurements had been matched precisely on the ground. The ramparts, it seemed, had been crafted with military precision, presumably overseen by engineers, and carried out by skilled and experienced individuals.

Marcus had been working hard back at Dig HQ, incorporating the team's findings into his three-dimensional model of the defences. Digital reconstructions often provide an aerial view of a site, which is handy for the archaeologist because we can compare it with maps and plans, but which – if you

think about it – is also rather odd, because it is a perspective that nobody would ever have witnessed at the time. Marcus's reconstruction brilliantly illustrated the importance of seeing things from many different perspectives, as he demonstrated to Hugh.

When viewed from above, the complex form of the town defences were perfectly apparent, but when Marcus switched the viewpoint to that of an enemy soldier approaching them from ground level, they were barely visible at all. And therein lay the true cunning of the design: the multiple lines of defence were almost invisible to the would-be attacker. There was no way of knowing

Finds

Marcus explains his model to Hugh

'Good job,' said Hugh, impressed

what obstacle you would face next, or where the defending soldiers might be hiding. Any army that wanted to breach the defences would have first had to sacrifice huge numbers of men to a terrifying, disorienting, and bloody end.

Through our ongoing work since leaving the site, we now suspect that the expansion of the moat would have been a deliberate tactic to prevent artillery from getting too close to the wall-line,

A soldier approaching the bastion would have very little chance of seeing what lay in store for them

The aerial perspective provides archaeologists with an understanding of how our findings relate to historical maps and plans

Parapet

Rampart

The soldiers used a timber framework to reinforce their earthwork defences

and to create a vast killing ground for any advancing infantry. Yet the space taken up by the expanded moat must have had a knock-on effect on other elements of the design, leaving us with questions about the size and function of the bastion.

Our work at King's Lynn was only the beginning, and I hope that David Flintham and the wonderful members of the King's Lynn Under Siege project will be able to carry on answering old questions and raising new ones, for many years to come.

Animal Bones

Reference bones at Dig HQ

Specialists in the field known as zooarchaeology often possess collections of carefully-treated and cleaned bones with which to compare their finds, and they conduct extensive research into published examples, too. For the rest of us, there's no substitute for all this experience and research, but it's still important to be able to broadly categorise what we find. Want to know your bird from your small mammal, or be able to recognise butchery marks? Let's get started!

Mammals Most people new to animal bones tend to underestimate the size of the original animal – I call it the 'wet dog' effect, as we're more used to seeing them with flesh and fur on! Ensure that you measure any bones you find and check them against known databases. Bear in mind, however, that size can vary greatly: some cattle may be larger than horses, for example, and there is an enormous range between different breeds of dog (think chihuahua vs. mastiff!).

Bony Pointers from Dr Hannah Russ

"In terms of texture, I like to think of mammal bones as being like an Aero bar, whereas fish bone is more like a Flake – it's almost wood-like. Bird bones are hollow, except for those from female birds during their egg-laying period, when they have the medullary bone, which looks a bit like the inside of a Crunchie. If you find a hollow bone with a 'double tube' appearance, though, it belonged to an amphibian."

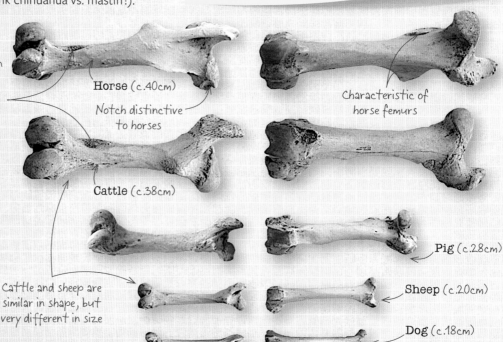

Supracondylar fossa: very large in horses, small but distinct in cattle and sheep, almost flat in pigs, absent in dogs

Horse (c.40cm)

Notch distinctive to horses

Characteristic of horse femurs

Cattle (c.38cm)

Example lengths of mammal femurs (upper leg bone)

Cattle and sheep are similar in shape, but very different in size

Pig (c.28cm)

Sheep (c.20cm)

Dog (c.18cm)

Birds and Fish

Birds and Fish As mentioned above, bird bones are mostly hollow. The most distinctive are the *carpometacarpus* in the wing (look out for the 'safety pin' shape!) and the *tarsometatarsus* in the leg, which has a claw-like end where the foot bones attach.

The most recognisable fish bones are the vertebrae, which look like little cylinders or cotton reels. For identifying the type of fish, the most useful bones are the four bones of the mouth.

How did the bones get there?

Common scenarios:

• **Pet burial.** A complete or near complete, articulated (i.e. bones where they should be) skeleton, with a grave cut (sharp change in the soil where the grave was dug and then filled in).

• **Food waste.** In a layer containing other discarded rubbish (e.g. broken pottery, various animal bones). Evidence for cut marks on the bones.

Carrier Pigeon skeleton

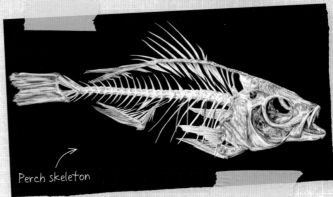

Perch skeleton

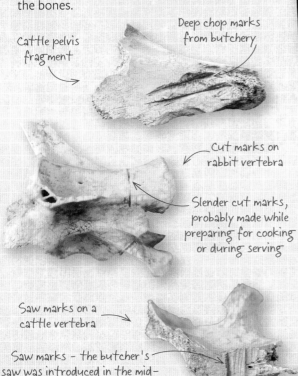

Cattle pelvis fragment

Deep chop marks from butchery

Cut marks on rabbit vertebra

Slender cut marks, probably made while preparing for cooking or during serving

Saw marks on a cattle vertebra

Saw marks – the butcher's saw was introduced in the mid-18th century, so saw marks can help to date the bones

---

WANT TO KNOW MORE?

These online resources are packed with reference material:

• Mammals: https://russellbone atlas.wordpress.com
• Small mammals: https://ifeelitinmybones.wordpress.com/2016/01/12/small-mammal-skeletal-comparison
• Fish: http://fishbone.nottingham.ac.uk
• Birds: https://www.royalbc museum.bc.ca/Natural_History/Bones/Introduction.htm
• Bird skulls: https://www.skullsite.com/

There was something rather magical about our time in the market town of Odiham. Throughout the week, we were repeatedly visited by a little robin, who hopped in and out of the trenches, quite unperturbed by our presence. And then there was – for want of a better way to describe it – a certain *stillness* to the air. It felt almost as though the place was holding its breath.

And after all, perhaps it was. Having waited so long for somebody to come and tease out its secrets, was Odiham delighted, or fearful that we were here at last, and ready to do just that? If it was fearful, then it was not without reason, because history tells us that it is likely to have kept some dark secrets in its time. We had come to seek evidence for

'Odiham Place', a long-lost Tudor hall that in the late 16th century was home to Sir Francis Walsingham, a powerful statesman and Queen Elizabeth I's 'spymaster', who ran a network of agents throughout Europe and orchestrated – among other things – the downfall and

The warmth and antiquity of Odiham

The robin

execution of Mary, Queen of Scots.

We met Hugh on the high street of this bustling market town, to explain why we were so interested in this place. We didn't know the origins of the house, but we had documentary evidence that it was here by the 1560s, when Queen Elizabeth visited it on a 'progress'. A progress is basically a Tudor version of a royal tour, albeit with rather less of the old, 'ah hello, and what do *you* do, then?' Our next piece of evidence for the house comes from a map sketched by one William Godson in 1739, almost 150 years after Walsingham's death.

We wanted to know what the house would have looked like in Walsingham's day, and how it might have changed over time. The houses of the ruling classes in Tudor England had an H-shaped (earlier) or E-shaped (later) plan, while the lower classes lived in simpler square or rectangular dwellings. The image on the map is a little ambiguous and, despite showing a house of some panache, it seems a touch on the small side. We knew that this was one of several properties Walsingham would have owned, but even so, would a smallish hall befit his status as one of the most powerful men in the country?

One possible explanation for the discrepancy was that the map only showed half of the house, as had been the case for us at Beningbrough in Yorkshire. I wasn't convinced by this idea, but it was important

'It's never been excavated, so this should be a really **rich** site to dig,' said our Rich, punning on his own name

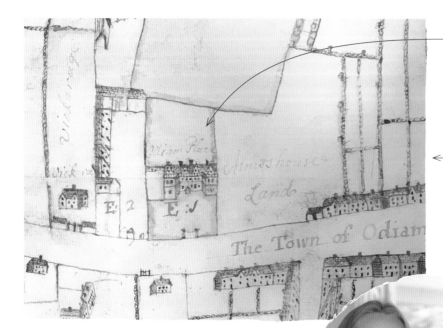

Our only clue to the appearance of the house was painted almost 150 years after Walsingham's death

Godson's map, sketched in 1739

I'm not sure whether we charmed the residents, or they charmed us

to investigate it archaeologically. Tash volunteered to take this on with a carefully sited trench in the garden belonging to local residents Linda and Grahame. If it was twice the size, we could expect the house to extend out this far, and for us to pick up evidence for walls or internal floor surfaces. Richard was also hoping to find structure in Luke and Adrienne's garden, which should be just over the remains of the front part of the house.

Meanwhile, I partnered up with Robin (our archaeology team member, not the bird) to put a trench into the car park beside the Cross Barn, built in 1532 and the earliest brick barn in Hampshire. The Cross Barn would have stood at the same time as the house itself, so it was a pretty handy point of reference for the brickwork. Given our uncertainty over the hall's extent, there was a lot of potential to answer our questions here, and also we wanted to see whether we could find a substantial feature that had shown up during some previous survey work, possibly a buried wall?

Expert archaeologists Alice and Marina arrive on site to dig

'We're putting a trench in a car park. That has worked out for archaeologists before...'

'It's a bit of a "yes or no" trench!'

Hugh Sheppard

We used the digger to remove a thick layer of landscaping material that had been used to build up the height of the car park. Just as we were coming to the base of this, I was visited by local historian Hugh Sheppard. I had been very much looking forward to meeting Hugh, as he was a renowned mine of information on the house, having spent several years visiting the British Library and the Hampshire records office to piece together its history. As he pointed out, we might expect to find

HOW TO READ A BRICK BUILDING

Until the early 20th century, almost all brick walls were built with two rows of bricks laid side-by-side, in what we call a 'double-skin' or 'double-leaf' wall. In order to increase their strength, as well as to enable decorative brickwork, such walls combine 'stretchers' and 'headers' in various different patterns, known as 'bonds'.

Stretchers and headers are really the same bricks in most cases; the only difference lies in which way they are oriented. If you imagine a finished brick wall, the stretchers are the bricks that have been laid lengthwise (stretching!), with their long side visible in the final wall. Headers are those bricks that have been laid at right-angles to the stretchers, so that their short end is visible in the final wall. In most bricks, the header is half the length of the stretcher, which makes it easier to combine them in different patterns.

From the 1920s, brick buildings in the UK started to be built with cavity walls. Rather than laying the two lines of brick directly side by side, a gap was left between them, reducing damp penetration and improving insulation. This gap necessitated the use of Stretcher bond, where all bricks were laid lengthways. To compensate for the loss of strength and stability by not using Cross bonds, metal ties were introduced to hold the two lines of bricks

RIGHT Stretcher bond is a good sign that your building dates to the 1920s or later

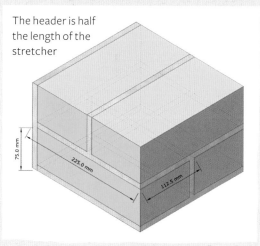

ABOVE The difference between a header and a stretcher depends on how it is placed in the wall

The header is half the length of the stretcher

75.0 mm   225.0 mm   112.5 mm

ABOVE Bricks are laid in different directions to increase the strength of the wall

Flemish bond

English bond

English Cross bond

English Garden Wall bond can have three or five courses of stretcher between each course of headers

together. Because Stretcher bond is almost exclusively associated with cavity walls, it is a pretty clear indication that your brickwork dates to the 1920s or later.

Older buildings were constructed with a variety of bonds, and some of the more common ones you may encounter are listed here. 'Flemish bond' alternates between stretchers and headers on each row: each stretcher is surrounded by four headers, and vice versa.

So-called 'English bond' sees alternating rows of stretchers and headers. When the gaps between the stretchers are not vertically aligned, this is known as 'English Cross bond'. Another variation on this is English Garden Wall bond, which typically has three or five courses of stretchers between each course of headers (when there are five courses, this is also known as 'American bond').

In older brickwork you may find the use of darker bricks as well as red ones, arranged to form particular patterns such as diamonds.

The 'H-shaped' Shaw House, built in 1581

The brickwork and windows of Shaw House

the kitchen in this area, which may have explained all the animal bones and oyster shells I was finding – evidence for fine dining!

This week, we were also joined by Dr Jonathan Foyle, architectural historian, who took Hugh off on a tour of the splendid surviving Tudor property of Shaw House in Berkshire. The house was built in 1581 by Thomas Dolman, whose family had made their fortune in the cloth industry. Keen to establish themselves within the landed aristocracy, who would have looked down on their 'new money', the house was built in the latest style, and is a fine example of Tudor architecture, with its characteristic H-shaped plan, its warm red bricks, and its large windows. Could there be the remains of such a grand building lying under Odiham today?

Upon returning from Berkshire, Hugh joined Robin and me in our car park trench, where we were making great archaeological progress, but slightly concerned about the disappearance of our little robin friend, who I had grown quite fond of. We were soon distracted, however, by the arrival of Hugh Sheppard, who ambled over to see how we were getting on.

As I showed the two Hughs, we had uncovered a beautifully preserved, enormous, curved brick structure. The narrow, handmade bricks were of the same dimensions as those in the Cross Barn, demonstrating that they probably date to the 16th century. What we had found was part of an enormous drainage system, just the sort of thing you would expect of a great house with large kitchens. After all, Elizabeth I did famously claim to

'Small market town, one of the great Queens of England - how do you square that?' asked Jonathan

have the heart and stomach of a king, and given her dad's reputation for banqueting, that was saying something!

Tash still hadn't come down onto any evidence for structure in her trench, but she was getting some beautiful 16th century finds, including a fragment of Tudor Green Glaze pottery. She took homeowner Linda along with her to Dig HQ to see whether Marcus Abbott could work his own brand of magic and recreate the pot. Because this

We uncovered the remains of an enormous culvert (drain)

Another clue - the top of this enormous culvert is visible in the brickwork on the other side of a more recent wall

Finds expert David Griffiths
identifies the Tudor Green Glaze

THE BIRTH OF ESPIONAGE

'What Walsingham's legacy really is, is MI5 and MI6 – the spy system – because he really is the first person in England to turn it into an art,' historian Dr Elizabeth Norton told Hugh.

In the later 16th century, the whole of Europe was being rocked by religious change, centring on the conflict between the Catholic Church in Rome, and the new Protestant versions of Christianity that opposed it. Earthly and heavenly power were bound up together in the minds of most people, and so matters of the soul were also very much matters of politics and state. On top of this, there was a monumental struggle between the sea-faring nations of western Europe over control of the Americas, which Europeans had only made contact with in the

piece didn't have any remains of the rim or base on it, it was difficult to pin down exactly which of the known forms of Tudor Green Glaze it originally came from, so instead Marcus created a beautiful little tableau for Linda, showing her the lot! And who knows, somewhere in her garden there may be more fragments awaiting discovery.

As delighted as she was with the reconstruction, Tash was desperate to get back to her trench and answer the question of whether the house extended this far. Taking down a smaller section within her trench to get a sense of how deep any structural evidence might be, Tash finally hit upon the goods.

preceding century, but which they were keen to exploit for material gain.

Elizabeth I, the 'Virgin Queen', was the last in line of Henry VIII's three legitimate heirs, and came to the throne in 1558 at the age of 25. Her claim to the throne rested entirely on the rejection of the Catholic Church, as it was this that had seen Henry VIII able to divorce his first wife and marry her mother, Anne Boleyn. Historical hindsight tells us that Elizabeth I was one of the longest-reigning monarchs of England, but at the time her grip on power would have felt far more shaky.

This is why Walsingham was so important to the Queen. She could be certain that he would remain loyal, as he was an avowed Protestant who had fled the country under the rule of her Catholic sister Mary I. He built up a network of spies across Europe, teasing out Catholic conspiracies, and obtaining information about enemy countries including Spain. In these times, torture was used as a means of extracting information from people, which is one reason the house may have held some truly dark secrets. Walsingham had other arrows in his quiver, however, and he made

ABOVE Tudor historian Dr Elizabeth Norton shows Hugh how messages were hidden in innocent-looking letters

a particular speciality of working with skilled code-breakers.

It was this shadowy network and use of code-breaking that Walsingham employed to entrap the main threat to Elizabeth's grip on the throne: her cousin, Mary Stuart (known to history as Mary, Queen of Scots). Mary had been forced to abdicate her throne in Scotland, and had fled to England to seek the protection of her cousin Elizabeth. As a Catholic, however, she was also a rallying point for rebellion, and so her 'protection' was more akin to imprisonment.

Walsingham wanted to remove the threat of Mary once and for all, and so he set about entrapping her with a carefully-planned plot. Using his underground network, he cut off all lines of communication outside of her prisons bar one, which he controlled. Mary's letters were intercepted and decoded by Walsingham's agents, until she finally sent the letter that was to condemn her and result in her execution for treason in October 1586.

Digital reconstruction expert Marcus wasn't sure which form the small fragment of pottery belonged to, so he put together a selection of the possibilities

more modest house was in keeping with its strategic location between key channels of communication from London to the south coast.

Richard also had something to reveal in Luke and Adrienne's garden: here, he had come down upon a thick layer of rubble from some large-scale demolition. The bricks, tiles and pottery fragments he found within this dense, compact layer were all of the appropriate date for the house. Richard was convinced that they were looking down at the house itself, albeit highly messed up –

A cobbled surface, almost certainly from a yard, told us that we weren't digging inside the house here, lending weight to our doubts about the house having been larger than shown on the map. Jonathan was particularly satisfied with this answer: he felt that a

Tash's cobbles suggested a yard surface

'Walsingham's home in puree form' as Hugh put it.

Hugh Sheppard, meanwhile, had been doing some digging of his own in the archives. He had found a lesser-known map dating to 1595, in which it was stated that the house had been commissioned not by Elizabeth I, but by Henry VIII, who had died in 1547. Its location next to a deer park implied that it was originally intended as a hunting lodge. We were starting to draw a picture of a far smaller and more modest house, built to a simple medieval hall design rather than a complex Elizabethan floorplan. But what did all this mean for our large drainage ditch in my car park trench?

The answer was in the archaeological layers: the stratigraphy. Based on the finds within the layers, we were able to date them, and to show the sequence of events over time. The lowest layer dated to the medieval period, before the house was built, with a 16th century layer of material above. If the culvert was there in Walsingham's day, we would expect the 16th century layer to lie on top it, but that wasn't what the archaeology suggested.

'It's not about a big house, showing off – it's the strategic location here'

Where the earlier layers were removed so the culvert could be installed

This layer lies over the culvert so it is more recent

16th century layer

Medieval layer

Small, discreet and perfect for dark dealings... and that's just the house

It's back to the drawing board for Odiham Place

Hugh's Hugh?

In fact, we had evidence that somebody had cut *through* these medieval and 16th century layers in order to install the huge drainage system. The house must have gone through a large structural change at some point after Walsingham's death, and before the Godson map was drawn.

Hugh, Marcus and Jonathan gathered together in Dig HQ to discuss the implications of all our new information. Our findings had confirmed that Godson's map was probably fairly accurate. The base plan of the house was of a medieval hall design, whereas the top parts such as the gables were consistent with the 1620s and 1630s, after Walsingham's death, when English architecture started to imitate Dutch trends.

In Walsingham's time, the strategic location and modest size of the house would have been useful for conducting the shadowy business of espionage, or holding sensitive

Privy Council meetings away from prying eyes. But in the 17th century, when it became a family residence, and needed large kitchens and appropriate drainage systems, the house underwent major remodelling.

The robin came back at the end of the week and irritated Robin by standing on the spoil heap and not budging. After much grumpy 'shooing', human Robin gave up and flung his spoil to the other side of the tarp, muttering something about 'these Tudors' and 'bloody birds'.

Still, I thought I caught the edge of a smile as he turned away to shovel.

The defiant robin returns

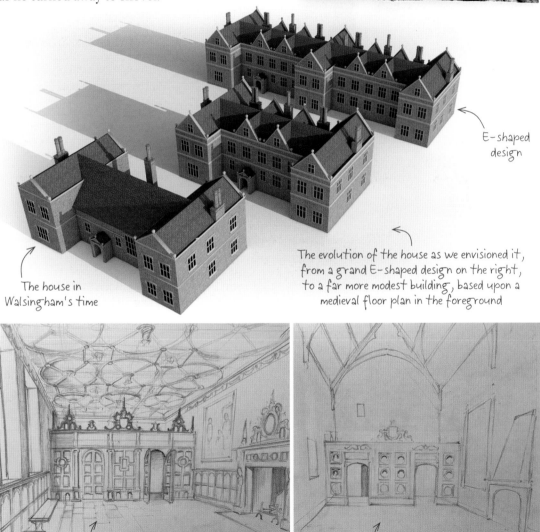

E-shaped design

The house in Walsingham's time

The evolution of the house as we envisioned it, from a grand E-shaped design on the right, to a far more modest building, based upon a medieval floor plan in the foreground

The interior of Shaw House – a 'new build' Elizabethan house

If the house was rebuilt over medieval footings, it could be expected to look something like this on the interior

CARING FOR FINDS

Archaeological 'finds' are portable objects relating to human activity, and are distinct from structural features such as walls. Finds are typically classified based on what they're made of. Common categories include pottery, animal bone, shell, metals, worked stone, glass and CBM (ceramic building material, e.g. bricks, tiles).

The first rule of Finds Club is that you must always label your finds to show which context they came from. Have a labelled finds tray ready before you start to excavate a new deposit or fill, and pop the finds in there as you work.

There are a few exceptional circumstances to bear in mind:

• If you come across potentially dangerous finds such as asbestos (see page 81) or incompletely decomposed animal remains, you should stop digging immediately.

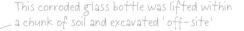
This corroded glass bottle was lifted within a chunk of soil and excavated 'off-site'

• If you find anything particularly special or unusual, leave it in place while you record its location and take a couple of photographs.
• Very delicate or fragile finds, such as severely corroded metal or glass, can be lifted along with the whole chunk of soil in which they are embedded and carefully excavated at your leisure.

Finds are typically kept together with other material from the same context. These are known in archaeology as **bulk finds**. Particularly unusual or informative finds are termed **small finds**, though they can be of any size. Bag small finds separately, and keep a register of any small finds in the back of your notebook. Give each one a

Excavating animal skeletons

You will need:
- a labelled finds tray or bag
- wooden digging tools such as lollipop sticks, skewers (see page 32)
- a soft brush for cleaning bones
- one or more sieves (if you have them)

If you happen upon an 'articulated' (intact) animal skeleton, you may want to try your hand at exposing it as fully as possible so that you can photograph it, before you go ahead and lift the bones from the ground. If you have a sieve, pass the soil through it to help catch any tiny bones you might have missed.

As you expose the skeleton, use the archaeological context to do some detective work: was the animal buried in a purpose-dug grave or pit, or are there other finds within the fill to suggest a different story?

Once you have exposed as much of the skeleton as you can, take some photographs. At least one of the photos should include a tape or ruler to provide scale, a label to identify the context number, and an indication of which way is north (trowels make excellent ad hoc arrows).

Whatever you do, please check the location of past pet burials with other members of your household BEFORE opening your trench, to avoid marching in through the back door with the remains of Gran's beloved Mr Whiskers held aloft in a plastic bag.

The mesh size of your sieve should be smaller than the finds you hope to catch

number (SF01, SF02, etc) and note which context it was in, its depth, and its distance from the south and west sides of the trench. At the other extreme, if you are pulling out masses of similar bricks, or lump after lump of mortar, then you should only collect a representative **sample** of these.

Butchered bone, fragments of pottery, and shell made up the bulk finds in this context

Cotton buds, either dry or slightly dampened, are fantastic for cleaning delicate or friable finds that wouldn't take kindly to a dunking

CLEANING FINDS

I can still remember standing in a Greek *apothíki* at the tender age of 21, watching open mouthed as a rack of the sort of pottery finds that would make the news if they turned up on a British dig were subjected to a strong dose of the power-hose.

These days, people are somewhat more cautious about cleaning finds, as we develop more and more ways to extract information from the things we recover, from microscopic scars indicating how a tool was used, to traces of pigment on ancient statues.

While I would not advocate the use of a power-hose, in most cases it is perfectly reasonable to clean the soil off your finds by the simple expedient of some fresh tap water and a (soft) toothbrush, leaving them to dry on layers of kitchen towel or old newspapers. Change the

water frequently, discarding the dirty water outdoors to avoid silting up your plumbing. It's really important to ensure that your finds don't get mixed up with those from other contexts, so change the water before washing finds from another context, and make sure they have labels with them while they're drying. The following should not be washed by this method:

• Anything with traces of pigment (e.g. painted plaster)
• Metals
• Friable (easily crumbled), prehistoric pottery
• Glass if highly corroded

RESEARCHING AND REPORTING FINDS

This is where the really exciting part begins! You can use the ID Guides in this book as starting points, but when it comes to research, the internet really is your oyster ... even if you want to research, well, oysters*.

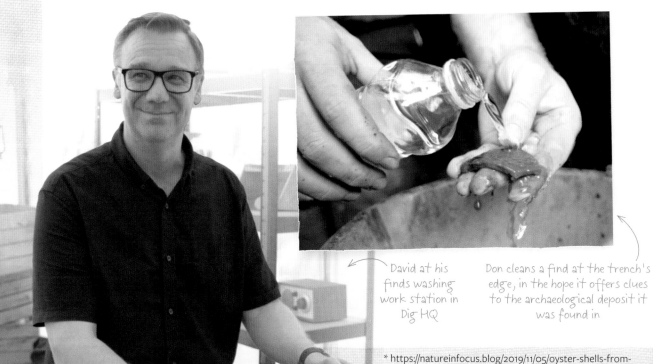

David at his finds washing work station in Dig HQ

Don cleans a find at the trench's edge, in the hope it offers clues to the archaeological deposit it was found in

* https://natureinfocus.blog/2019/11/05/oyster-shells-from-archaeological-sites-a-brief-illustrated-guide-to-basic-processing

Taking measurements of a tile for comparison with examples from other sites →

In England and Wales, anything dating to earlier than the mid-17th century (and certain more recent finds) can be reported to the Portable Antiquities Scheme. This vast online database provides a crucial resource for amateur and professional researchers. If you think you have found something eligible for the scheme, the first step is to get in touch with your local Finds Liaison Officer (FLO), who will assess whether your finds meet the requirements for reporting to the scheme: https://finds.org.uk/contacts

STORAGE AND CONSERVATION

Among the treasures found in the tomb of Egyptian pharaoh Tutankhamun when it was opened in 1922 was a vast array of pristine wooden objects. Yet even as the tomb's excavators worked to recover the objects for conservation, they reported eerie creaking sounds coming from the wood; tell-tale signs that it was rapidly succumbing to environmental stress, and a clear illustration of the danger of change when it comes to preserving finds.

Finds are at their most vulnerable at the point of excavation, but even afterwards you should keep an eye on the following risks:

- Sunlight (especially damaging to pigments)
- Oxygen (corrosive, particularly in combination with moisture)
- Moisture (especially bad for metals, glasses)
- High temperature (or greatly fluctuating temperature)
- Pests (rats, mice, cockroaches, fungi, mites)
- pH (extremes of acid or alkali and/or change from the burial environment)

If you notice signs of deterioration in your finds, and want to keep them out of harm's way, a sealable plastic box lined with acid-free paper and kept somewhere cool, dry, and out of the reach of sunlight and pests should work well for most finds. Just remember to label it!

Corroded glass often takes on an attractive, iridescent appearance

Rust, the product of iron corrosion, can grow around the original object, making its form difficult to determine without specialist kit such as X-ray scanners

14 PREHISTORIC MYSTERIES

▶ STRETTON, EAST STAFFORDSHIRE ◀

Richard, Tash and I tracked Hugh down to a charming farm shop just outside of Stretton in East Staffordshire, where we found him casually sipping a fruit smoothie and soaking in the warmth of a fine day. I must confess that I noticed a somewhat Hugh-ish look pass over his face when we appeared; a sort of weary acceptance that we were about to drag him away from his creature comforts to some unknown muddy garden.

A real smoothie... and he's holding a delicious fruit drink!

Still, he couldn't be too disappointed with what we had in store for him. In a real first for *The Great British Dig*, our investigation was taking us all the way back to prehistory, to the many thousands of years of human life in Britain before the Romans turned up and started to write down what they encountered (well, their version of it, anyway). Britain's prehistoric inhabitants surrounded themselves with a rich, diverse material world, but because most of it was made of things that perish rather quickly in the ground, much of our best evidence comes from subtle changes in soil texture and colour.

Back in the 1950s, a series of photographs had been taken from the air over Stretton, and they showed up some rather intriguing marks in the fields. A strange series of small dark patches ran in a long straight line, while elsewhere there were clusters of enormously large circles. It was not until the 1980s, after the fields had been built over with houses, that the photos were re-examined and recognised for what they were: evidence for buried archaeology.

Based on excavations elsewhere in Britain, we could be fairly confident that the circular shapes were the remains of roundhouses, but we didn't know whether they still survived. As our prehistoric expert Dr Caroline Pudney explained to Hugh, for almost 3,000 years, from the start of the Early Bronze Age in 2400 BC until well into the Roman occupation of southern Britain, people here lived in circular dwellings, setting them apart from most of continental Europe. They varied hugely, from the wattle-and-daub roundhouses of the lowlands to the drystone brochs of western Scotland, but always, it seems, the circular form was key.

I have often wondered about the meaning of that emphasis on circular, rather than linear dwellings. Perhaps they began as a good way to build a solid structure, but surely they would have come to shape the worldview of the people who grew up in, built, repaired, slept, loved, ate, drank and died in the round. And how much, I think, must living and working in regular, boxy,

Our expert in prehistory, Dr Caroline Pudney, tells Hugh all about roundhouses

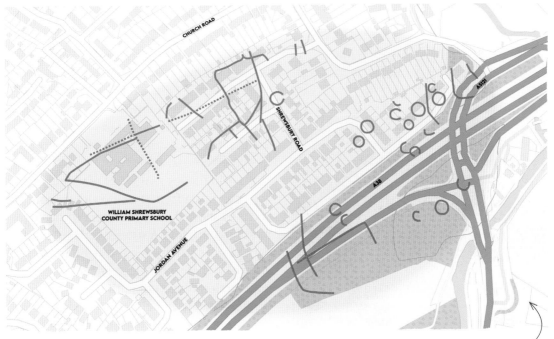
By linking the marks seen on the 1950s aerial photographs with more recent maps, we were able to work out which of today's gardens might have a roundhouse underneath them

All that usually survives of a prehistoric settlement (right) are traces of the houses' drainage ditches (below)

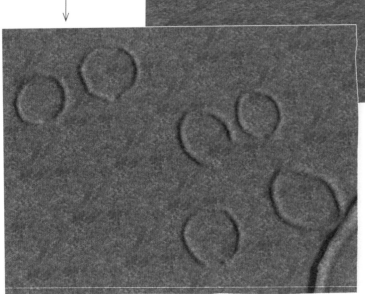

had shown that mysterious line of features. Based on evidence from other sites, we suspected that this was a series of Bronze Age pits, the function of which was somewhat mysterious, but which occasionally yielded extraordinary finds within their fills.

Headteacher Elaine was not only happy to let us to bring in a mechanical digger and open a large trench in her school's playing field, she was also excited about the prospect of lending a hand. Her work paid off, too, because early on in

partitioned buildings have shaped our worldview in the modern day.

Putting aside the symbolic aspects for a moment, the longevity of the roundhouse as a form meant one other thing: if we wanted to know whether this settlement was built in the Bronze Age, the Iron Age, or the Romano-British period, we were going to have to dig.

We were hoping that some prehistoric archaeology survived beneath the modern gardens, but we also had another ace up our sleeve: the large playing fields of William Shrewsbury Primary School, which lay where the old photographs

Pupils at William Shrewsbury school get stuck into digging up their playing field

AERIAL SURVEY

From the late 18th century, hot air balloons provided those who rode in them with an entirely new perspective: the world from above. Thanks to advances in photography over the following hundred years, it became possible to record this bird's eye view for posterity. Ultimately, however, it was the invention of the aeroplane in 1903 that finally propelled us into the era of aerial survey, and although our technologies have developed since then, the basic principles remain the same.

The canny archaeologist is able to spot things from the air that are difficult or nigh on impossible to pick up on at ground level:

SOIL MARKS appear in land that has been ploughed or eroded. Ploughing turns the soil on its head, bringing lower layers to the surface and allowing us to identify differences in the colour and water retention of the soil that indicate buried archaeological features.

CROP MARKS are a handy way of detecting buried archaeology in active agricultural land. Modern ploughs cut deep, destroying the upper layers of archaeology, but features below this line often give their presence away by the effect they have on the crops.

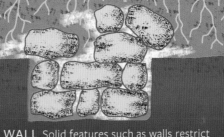

DITCH Buried ditches and pits allow longer root growth and retain water, so these plants are taller and more drought-resistant

WALL Solid features such as walls restrict root grown, so the plants are shorter and more susceptible to drought

(continued overleaf)

LEFT Parch marks reveal the buried wall foundations of Tixall Hall, Staffordshire, in 2018

BELOW Crop marks reveal the two large ditches of an Iron Age enclosure near South Wonston, Hampshire

PARCH MARKS appear in crops and other vegetation such as lawns during time of drought, when buried features restrict root growth and prevent plants above them from reaching the water table.

EARTHWORKS are archaeological remains that stand above ground. These include deliberate earthen constructions, such as burial mounds, but the trained eye can also detect surface undulations that indicate there are buried walls and ditches beneath.

The use of LiDAR coupled with historical mapping in the New Forest National Park Authority has led to the identification of over 3,000 sites, two-thirds of which were previously unknown

In 1972, the Landsat-1 satellite became the first to map the Earth from space, thanks in part to an ingenious multispectral scanner designed by American physicist Virginia Norwood, scanning light waves from the visible spectrum to near-infrared. The resolution and spectral capabilities of satellite images have increased hugely over the years, and they are sought by the military, ecologists, and researchers in a vast range of fields besides.

Another major technological breakthrough came with the introduction

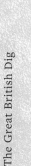

Researchers have used satellite imagery to help to locate historical shipwrecks, based on the sediment plumes they create

SS *Sansip*

SS *Samvurn*

of so-called 'LiDAR', which uses a clever combination of lasers and computational algorithms to create high resolution 3-dimensional maps of landscapes and objects. What is more, LiDAR can 'see' beneath vegetation, even dense woodland, providing clues to truly hidden and mysterious sites.

In spite of technological advances, older aerial imagery is still really important in tracing change over time, finding evidence for loss or destruction of archaeological heritage, and in detecting sites that only show up in certain conditions, such as drought.

WANT TO GO FURTHER?

When it comes to aerial archaeology, the sky's the limit! But here are some great ways to make a start:

- **Google Earth Pro** is free to download, and the desktop version includes a 'historical imagery' feature (the little clock icon)
- **Britain from Above** features an interactive map of more than 95,000 early 20th century aerial photographs across Britain – pretty handy for exploring your local area: **britainfromabove.org.uk**
- Fancy dipping into a massive archive of declassified US spy imagery from the 1960s and early '70s? Check out: **corona.cast.uark.edu**
- Satellite coverage today is so enormous that researchers often turn to citizen science projects to request public assistance. Here's a recent example: **globalxplorer.org/expedition**

The Great British Dig

Stretton resident Mangal and I opening a trench in his stunning garden

the dig we hit upon our first ancient find, and it was a beaut! A significant chunk of Roman wall plaster, complete with painted red decoration, was our first confirmation that this area had been occupied for far longer than its earliest appearance in historical records, in 1327. As pointed out by finds expert Dr Hannah Russ, such a well-preserved piece was unlikely to have travelled too far from its original location, suggesting that there had once been a pretty

fancy building in the area.

So, we had some pretty good evidence that this area was occupied during the Roman period, but were people living here before they arrived? Tash called Hugh over to one of the back garden trenches, where she had been working with 6-year-old Willow. It took Hugh a little while to get to the bottom of Tash's visible excitement, but eventually she revealed the cause: a rim fragment, from a type of pottery associated with the Iron Age. Because it was fired in a bonfire rather

By the look on Willow's face, Tash might just have inspired another future archaeologist!

Much to my delight, finds expert Hannah confirms that we found Roman wall plaster

Fine Roman plaster from a decorated wall

Traces of red paint

than a kiln (see page 28), prehistoric pottery does not always survive very well in Britain, so it was a lucky find indeed, and it was our first sign that the settlement pre-dated the Romans.

'Two and a half thousand years old, and in your garden,' remarked Hugh to Willow.

'Older than Daddy,' she replied, sagely.

As fantastic as the pottery fragment was, nobody was having much luck with detecting evidence for buildings in the gardens. Had it been destroyed when the houses were built, or had we missed it with our trench locations?

The difficulty with trying to find prehistoric archaeology in people's back gardens is that it is so intangible. These roundhouses would have been made by driving large timber posts

'It's unbelievable' – Tash with the rim from an Iron Age pot

Caroline shows Hugh around a reconstruction roundhouse at Beeston Castle

In all but the most exceptional circumstances, the only structural traces left to archaeology are different soil textures where the drainage ditches and post-holes were eventually filled in, burnt traces where the hearth had been, and sometimes the remains of charcoal and burnt daub, if the house had been lost to fire.

We were having more luck with our search for the line of pits in the school playing field. As we first cleaned back the soil, several darker patches appeared, showing the location of the pits, but once the sun had been on them for a while, they disappeared before our eyes. Going in with trowels, we could easily feel the soil changes, but to get a sense of the bigger picture, I co-opted Hugh to sprinkle the soil with a hosepipe. The

into the ground to support the roof and doorway, with walls of wattle (a lattice of thin branches) and dried daub (clay, dung, and straw), and thatched roofs, with circular 'drip-ditches' running around the outside to help drain away the rainwater. A central hearth was the hub of family life, the focus of cooking, and a source of light for indoor craft activities.

principle is similar to the way soil and crop marks are made: whatever filled in the pits is less compact than the soil they were dug into, so it takes more water and 'pops' out visually. Lest you doubt my word, you have it from TV's Hugh Dennis himself, that the soil changes are 'very obvious, once you start scraping'.

The contents of those pits was going to be incredibly informative, so rather than throwing the soil we took out onto the spoil heap, we sent it over to Don in Dig HQ, where he combined it with water and passed it through sieves of various sizes, looking for any tiny things we would have missed while digging. He found fragments of pottery, the waste flakes where stone tools had been struck, and best of all, some surviving seeds and grains, which he showed to me. The seeds were from typical weeds that grow on well-manured

It is often easier to feel the changes in the soil than to see them

soils; a good sign that we were dealing with agricultural lands. The products of those lands was confirmed by the presence of some wheat grains: beer and bread.

Over on the other side of Dig HQ, Richard had arrived with a challenge for digital guru Marcus: to reconstruct the Iron Age pot that Tash's rim fragment had belonged to. Having laid down the gauntlet, or rather, the rim, Richard ambled off, returning later to check out the results. Marcus had used a diameter

Hugh wets the soil to help show up the prehistoric features

Don wet sieves the soil on the hunt for tiny finds

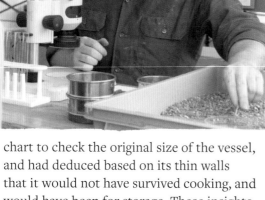

Don with his fine-mesh sieves

Don shows me the fruits (or should I say, grains?) of his sieving

chart to check the original size of the vessel, and had deduced based on its thin walls that it would not have survived cooking, and would have been for storage. These insights, coupled with some research into examples from elsewhere, provided enough evidence to reconstruct the entire pot.

Satisfied with his results, Richard came to lend a hand in the school playing fields. He joined expert archaeologist Marina in excavating the fills of the pits we had exposed in one half of the trench, while the rest of the team worked to clean up the other half, to see if the line continued. Richard's luck was in, as his pit yielded a fragment of a stone blade, confirmed by Hannah and Caroline

to date to the Middle Bronze Age. It seemed that we had been correct about the date of our pits!

Up at the other end of the trench, we were in for a real surprise, as we exposed something that hadn't been at all visible on the aerial photographs, so I called over Hugh and Elaine to take a look. Chivvying the unsuspecting Elaine to a spot towards the edge of the trench, I explained to her that she was standing in the middle of a roundhouse!

There was no mistaking the characteristic shape of the drip-ditch that would have surrounded the building, and although it ran into the side of the trench, enough survived for us to estimate the diameter of the house

Richard shows Hugh his remarkable Bronze Age find

at 8 metres. An overjoyed Elaine pointed to the Year 3 classroom window, where her pupils had been studying the Iron Age, all the time unaware that they had their very own roundhouse just under the playing fields!

Upon excavating it, we discovered that the drip-ditch had been cut into some of the pit features we were still digging elsewhere in the trench. Knowing our pits to be Bronze Age in date, we were able to confirm that the house itself was built in the Later Bronze Age or the Iron Age.

The school playing fields had one more surprise in store for us. Right at the base of one of the pits, Marina uncovered a truly extraordinary find: a beautiful, symmetrical arrowhead, expertly struck from flint. Up in Dig HQ, Caroline confirmed for us that the arrowhead was even older than Richard's

Richard challenges Marcus to reconstruct an Iron Age pot...

...and with some clever deduction, Marcus succeeds

Projecting the full diameter of the roundhouse

Elaine discovers that she's standing inside a prehistoric roundhouse

blade, and dated to the Early Bronze Age, around 4,500 years ago.

It is tempting to assume that as soon as metal became available, people would have abandoned their stone tools, but the technology of knapping (striking) fine-grained stone to create predictable fractures and sharp edges continued throughout the Bronze Age. And why not? It was certainly far easier to get hold of than the copper and tin required to make bronze.

BARB – originally there would have been two barbs on this arrowhead, designed to ensure it stayed in the prey's flesh

Marina calls me over to see the barbed and tanged flint arrowhead

TANG – for hafting onto the shaft of the arrow

The girls could not believe there was an ancient house under their playing field

Our time in Stretton had passed like a dream. Unexpected roundhouses and evidence for posh Roman buildings were glittering treasures finds indeed, but personally, I was lost in the wonder of that long line of Bronze Age pits, which at other sites have been interpreted as boundary markers. How strange, then, that they were not a high fence or earthen bank, but a series of *pits* dug into the ground, with objects hidden away in them. Perhaps this was a spiritual, or magical boundary. Perhaps people in the Bronze Age saw other worlds intertwined with their own; worlds that even archaeology cannot hope to retrieve. But by coming here, and allowing archaeology to open our eyes, we can at least remind ourselves that they existed.

A peaceful day on the farm in Iron Age Stretton, as visualised by Marcus Abbott

CARRY ON DIGGING!

Confession time: I'm a bit of weirdo, as it happens. The chances are that if you have read this far, you've already come to that conclusion independently, but honestly, I think most archaeologists are rather odd. I'm not sure whether we go into archaeology because we're odd, or whether it is archaeology that makes us that way, but what I do know is that we see things differently to most people.

Take an archaeologist on a walk and they will read the landscape as somebody else might read the Sunday papers. Ask an archaeologist to examine the contents of your rubbish bin, and they will extract a unique perspective on your life, and the world we live in today. 'Marry an archaeologist,' said Agatha Christie, because the older you get, the more interesting they'll find you (and she should know; she did).

You might ask, who are these strange archaeologists? Are they people who have studied the subject at university? People who earn their living by digging trenches or studying finds? The answer, I believe, is that if you have read, engaged with, and enjoyed this book,

then you are an archaeologist.

We archaeologists are all those who actively seek to learn about our shared human story through the material things that past people left behind. Like historians, we are interested in words, but our connection with the past runs far deeper. To be an archaeologist is to feel the electric thrill of recovering an object that was last touched by human hands hundreds, even thousands of years ago. To be an archaeologist is to question everything you see around you, and to ask yourself how it got there. To be an archaeologist is to be a wanderer, an adventurer, a detective, and a storyteller.

Welcome.

Free online resources

There are many ways to continue your voyage into archaeology that won't cost you a penny, as long as you have access to an internet connection at home or in your local library. The following online resources are just a selection of what is out there. Happy hunting!

Joining a local archaeology group is by far and away the best route into archaeology. The BAJR website hosts a map of such groups across the UK, with links to their homepages: www.bajr.org/whosewho/archsoc.asp

The Portable Antiquities Scheme hosts a range of great guides to identifying finds, and is the place to report your finds if you live in Wales or England: www.finds.org.uk/counties/findsrecordingguides

The Council for British Archaeology offers a wealth of advice on getting into archaeology: www.archaeologyuk.org/ways-into-archaeology

Dig It! is a hub for all sorts of resources on Scottish archaeology, and features guides to decoding some of the more complex and scientific aspects of archaeology: www.digitscotland.com/category/decoding-archaeology

Historic England have a large selection of guides available for download, many of which apply across the UK, although you'll have to do a bit of sifting because some of them are very specialised: www.historicengland.org.uk/advice/find/a-z-publications

BAJR guides are aimed at professional archaeologists in the UK, but they provide a fantastic introduction to a lot of useful topics: www.bajr.org/BAJRread/BAJRGuides

SCRAN is a website hosted by Historic Environment Scotland, with access to a huge range of resources: www.scran.ac.uk

Internet Archaeology is a research journal in which every article is freely available to read and download: www.intarch.ac.uk

Potted History is a fantastic place to learn more about pottery: www.pottedhistory.co.uk

ACKNOWLEDGEMENTS

This book would not be complete without thanking all the wonderful local communities who have welcomed us so warmly, and who put up with our muddy footprints all over their beautiful lawns. You have been incredible, and you make the show what it is.

Nor would it have been possible without a whole bunch of on- and off-screen talent. Thanks are due to my co-hosts Tash Billson, for all the times you've infected me with the giggles, and your general excellence, and to

Richard Taylor; you're fab, and you really do give the best hugs. Mr Hugh Dennis, it has been a genuine pleasure to work with you, and since you have been so kind, it's only right to confess that it was Jim and me who changed your name to 'Huge Pennis' on that sandwich bag – sorry.

Don O'Meara, it's good to have a porpoise in life, so keep jousting, and I'll see you at the open mic. David Griffiths, you're simply a brick, which is also the main line of your theme tune (it's a work in progress). Hannah Russ, my favourite reverse minion, you are the bee's knees and the fish's scales. To the many other specialists who lent us their expertise, and managed not to kill our star presenter during the off-sites (in spite of letting him handle various lethal weapons) it has been a genuine pleasure. This paragraph ends by recognising you, Marcus D. Abbott. You are the loveliest, kindest and most talented person I have ever met. Thank you for being in my life.

Behind the scenes of *The Great British Dig* is a huge bunch of incredibly gifted and hard-working people in production and crew, many of whom carry on long after we have stomped the mud off our boots and gone home. Audrey Neil, you are an icon, and you would still be my first choice for delivering the baby. Rich Mathews you are the cutest – keep on singing! Steve Wynne, you changed my life for the better, and I'm so grateful. Han Smith, forever united by our trauma bond from *that* day… we're the OGs, babes. Tom Benson-Geddes, for coming up with the idea for the show, and for being kinda hot in a Colin Farrell way – ta, mate.

Lucy Malins, Max Langton, Mike Ball and Nick Frend, gone but not forgotten – we missed you in Series 2. Alex Meacock, thank you for never droning on, and for always being a pleasure to work with. Myke Dunn, quick question – would you please voice

the trailer for the movie of my life? George Petias, you box of quotes and wonders, there are many things I would do to help you, and digging a hole in the wintry earth with my bare hands just so you can shoot a minute of footage that'll never make the edit is apparently one of them. Fergus Thom, you talented monster, will you ever have enough footage of bees in lavender?

Gareth Buss, Shane Gravestock, Rory Dunnings and Fraser Stone: sometimes it's hard to believe you're all grown-ups with proper jobs, but that's only because you make the long days so much more fun. To the lovely Paul Atkinson and Ben Goulding, for

every time you had to deal with kids shouting at you, or had to make hideously unreasonable requests of innocent members of the general public, thank you, you absolute darlings. Doug Krier, you gorgeous hunk, take me to one of your fancy parties! Emily Dias-Geoffrey and Meg Connolly, my younger sisters in our big TV family, and the most important people on set: you rock.

To all the runners who have made us tea, logged, shopped, driven, remembered the sunscreen and sat on boring tent duty – thank you, and I've loved getting to know you. To Tom Little and Geoff Bone, hope to catch you out and about sometime up here in the Toon. Thank you Cara Roxburgh for styling us, and for making Tash and me giggle when we accidentally glimpsed your notes on the presenters ('Richard = solid bloke'). All the editors and behind the scenes people who have to spend hours of their lives watching us, and whom we never get to meet – thanks so much (and um, make me look good, yeah?).

There are people who shine so brightly that they make everybody around them look good. That is our beautiful, talented Jane Barrie-Bramwell: we need you and we love you.

I'm enormously grateful to More4, Channel 4, and especially to Tim Hancock for believing in the show and steering us in the right direction. To Jim Brightman and Chris Scott, the twinkly-eyed Archaeology Mam and Dad of Solstice Heritage, thank you for finding such incredible sites and amazing team members.

My warmest thanks also to Jonathan Eyers and Stuart Cooper for guiding me through writing this book, and to everybody who worked on it at Bloomsbury, Strawberry Blond, and Solstice Heritage, especially dear Jim, my fellow-storyteller, who has done so much to help bring it to fruition. To Austin Taylor, for making the book look great, and putting up with relentless, and often conflicting feedback from the rest of us, thank you from the bottom of my pedantic little heart! Thanks too, to the illustrators who made my strange sketches of soil marks and Harris matrices look somehow comprehensible, and to proofreader Kristen Mankosa, who worked so hard and efficiently to turn things around in time.

The following individuals and institutions generously allowed us to reproduce their images: Hannah Russ of archaeology.biz;

The Great British Dig

Marcus Abbott; Graham Taylor of Potted History; The National Trust; Maria Court of The New Forest National Park Authority, the New Forest Higher Level Stewardship (HLS) scheme; and Lawrence Shawarma.

And now. It takes a village to raise a child. We wouldn't be able to do what we do, or to properly interpret and archive our findings, without all the unique and incredible professional archaeologists who turn up on site every day to dig, interpret and record the archaeology, and who stay behind to backfill. Your talent, humour, perseverance, and – in some cases – liver resilience are inspirational. Thank you from the bottom of my heart to all of you: Robin Taylor-Wilson, Ben Moore, Victoria Lucas, Eleonora Montanari, Nathan Berry, Clare Henderson, Alice Hall-Thomas,

Ayesha Purcell, Marina Vatylioti, Mandy Burns, Gulfareen Chohdry, Frankie Wildmun, Terry Frain, David Connolly, Paul Renner, Laura Parker, Scott Williams, Naomi Akintola and Gareth Davies. You are the unsung heroes and the true stars of the show.

PICTURE CREDITS

INDEX